Meditation for Badassery

Rock Your Mind

Rodasi Campbell

Edition Two

ISBN-13: 9798676240806

Cover design by: Rodasi Campbell + Robin Stremlow
Printed in the United States of America

This book is not meant to give professional advice
nor to offer any guarantees. This book is not meant
to diagnose or treat any mental or emotional
disorders. If you have a history of either of these,
please consult your care providers before beginning
the practices in this book.

Jai Ma

DEDICATIONS

Dedicated to The Divine Muse for giving me life and the fierce drive to find You.

For my daughters, Lauren + Elora.

For YOU, my fellow badass seekers-to-finders.

CONTENTS

PREFACE

Karma to Dharma (My Story)

"Get still inside and you'll see your whole life experience is an elaborate story you've wove, and the Real you is just enjoying the show."
- Derek Rydall

"The world, like a dream full of attachments and aversions seems real until the awakening." - Adi Shankaracharya

Age 18. My first meditation. I tried to clear my mind. I tried to watch thoughts like clouds. I tried to find peace. It didn't work on my own. I didn't have an effective tool or proper guidance.

So for some years I gave up - like many of you. Left to our own - invariably the voice in the head wins.

Intuitively, I somehow knew that Meditation was the only real salvation I would have in this lifetime. I had to figure out how to do it. Something in me would not accept that I wasn't cut out for it.

Have you ever had a moment on your knees where you were like, "screw you God, kill me now or show me THE WAY!"? That's where I was at and the call was answered.

In 1999, I took a few meditation classes and eventually was led to a weekend course. I discovered an ancient and effective practice. These meditative tools are used with eyes open as well closed.

I was taught by modern day monks - two women who had an inner peace that made them shine. Yet somehow they seemed quite normal too. I didn't understand what I was seeing, but I wanted what they had.

So with effective techniques on board and access to qualified, experienced guidance, I dove into practice. There were zero bells and whistles - no fluff, not glamour, no angels singing.

My suffering was not exactly removed, but I felt more comfortable in my own skin. I had a sense of being very on-point with what I was doing. So much so that I wound up applying for an immersive course of study at the same teacher training facility where my teachers had trained.

Deepening

I spent a year in service at this training facility in devotional yoga and meditation practices. I then entered into a 7-month training program where I was meditating at least 10-14 hours a day. That was the beginning of the greatest love affair of my life - with mySelf, with inner stillness, with the Divine.

I started yoga and meditation because I knew I was here for *something more*, but for me, there was a sense of urgency. I had to find it or I was going to die sooner than later.

The endless state of running from my inner stress, anxiety, fear, depression pushed me to find an experiential solution. By consistently meditating, I inadvertently stopped running, started being, and sat still long enough to fall in love.

I came to meditation to heal my pain, my life, and to become a better person. I found out that from the perspective of awakened consciousness, there was nothing wrong with me in the first place. Meditation saved my life in more ways than one.

I discovered that nothing needed fixing in order for me to know a living experience of love, peace, joy, purpose - of *badassery* right now. Who knew?

Interestingly, I didn't like that realization at first. I was very attached to my pain, drama, emotions and to the storylines of my life.

If you had said I was attached, I would have gone into some version of spiritual bypassing (go look it up if you don't know).

It wasn't conscious of course, or I may have been in a better position to admit it. It was unconsciously done to protect myself, to survive and to fake the appearance of thriving. Just like many folks I've met on this journey.

Holiness in Humanness

Over time, an ease, a gentleness, and an unshakable certainty locked in place. I became less and less interested in the movement of my mind, emotions and circumstances.

Greater degrees of willingness and capacity to be in a state of pure presence grew and stabilized. Less effort but still great commitment and devotion to practice have been and remain required.

I practiced meditation and being present through suicidal depression, alcoholism, addiction to attention and other forms of struggle and suffering.

I practiced as a single mom, an entrepreneur, a lover, as someone healing trauma, recovering from being an empath, and recovering from being a spiritual-seeker addict. I've come to a new state with access to true compassion, awareness, understanding, acceptance, and the capacity to be, sit still, stand in the fire, love.

I know why I exist. I know what my purpose is.

Training to Serve

At some point it hit my heart so fully that I had to share the news - *peace is here right now and it always has been!*

I had to let the people know: *Guys! There is nothing you need to heal about you or your life in order to know peace! All you have to do is get good at sitting still, at shifting your attention. Pay attention! OMG! Check it out!*

In 2010, I entered into a second training for the purposes of further stabilizing the presence of peace and love in life, but also to train to teach others these practices.

This second training was an International course taking place in Spain and the USA, both in-residence and distance, spanning about a year.

In studying with my teacher, I found the kind of certainty and confidence I never knew I needed. I found great freedom and humility both. I found great joy and other things that I thought were luxuries for the far more privileged than I.

Student-Teacher

Currently, I continue to discover more all of the time. I am totally still in training. I aspire to be so unwaveringly present that nothing ever out of habit or temptation takes the attention from the fullness of consciousness right now.

I'll continue exploring the present moment until this is so or die trying.

I am recovering from being an addicted seeker and becoming a playfully engaged and curious finder of what the Universe is presenting now, and now and now.

I am privileged to be in service to others while remaining an ongoing student myself. I get to share how it has gone so far living life evermore present.

I share the landmines that I, my peers, my students and clients have traversed. I celebrate intangible victories. I help direct those just beginning to hear the stirrings of desire for something more.

I help others to start a practice, a lifestyle, and I help to identify pitfalls and offer suggestions for moving ahead.

I give seasoned advice for how to cultivate, fortify and stabilize the new habits, awareness and state of consciousness emerging.

I have taught others going through many other types of life experiences. People who no longer have to try to be present, no longer struggle internally as they once did, people who now are locked into an unconditional sense of purpose.

I have watched as a few dozen of the thousands go on to become teachers themselves in service to this radical upgrade for humanity into the badassery of conscious evolution.

It absolutely rocks my mind, people.
Thank God for it all.

This opportunity to transcend these karmic issues in me and my ancestral lineage has provided depth to be offered to you.

Isn't that INCREDIBLE?

On another level, I personally feel like a goddamn miracle.

Because of this, there is a responsibility, privilege and a passion to serve other people in recognizing and cultivating the embodied state of badassery; beyond the lack-luster, drone-like existence of the average human.

My practice, my teacher, teaching others- it has gifted me with a whole lot of my days filled with peace, wholeness, passionate aliveness, purpose.

My capacity to dissolve into and stick around in this present moment evolves continuously as humanity evolves and as the experience of life changes.

From here, life is fascinating and purely magical like when I was a child. Not one part of it is better or holier than any other: The traumas and hardships of the past compared with sitting on the mountain in Spain in meditation with my teacher and peers - all of it Holy.

Now, is that something or what?

PROLOGUE

Your Birthright

We all begin in that state of union - of oneness. Life is magical and fluid for each of us early on.

At some point we learn from our environment that what we seek is out there somewhere, and further we are taught to seek it with our mind.

No one teaches us to maintain that relationship with oneness, intuitive living, non-resistance to what moves through us or is presented to us. No one teaches us that whatever we may seek, it is within us. No one teaches us to be super attentive and rest, still inside. No one tells us that resting inside is in fact where our salvation lies.

No one taught us that because humanity didn't know yet. At least most of humanity.

But we are now ushering in a new paradigm right here and now, folks. We have the opportunity to change this. You came here to do this. The karma you came in with and carry today is actually your purpose.

The Universe is SUPER smart and we are graced with the ability to seek, find, employ, develop and ultimately help others.

That is transmuting karma into dharma - being made useful and serving the Awakening.

Humans don't make that kind of true change in the mind. This kind of growth only happens from a shift in consciousness. Sustainable shifts in consciousness generally come from meditative practice.

If I can go from where I came from to where I'm at today, then SO CAN YOU. You just have to want to. This all may sound radical or even impossible. This kind of unconditional holiness was definitely not the experience at one time for me.

At one point this existence seemed like it was far off and reserved for the likes of Buddha, Jesus or my Teacher. It is no longer the case.

Even as the tides of life deliver varying degrees of intensity and apparent growth, I experience it all as the same thing - a state of divinity.

There is awareness of Self as inner-presence. There is also awareness of the appearance of movement of life.

Yet still, the notes of the Symphony of Life remain a precious privilege to witness in their rise and fall. These notes were once the only identification I had and so went the roller coaster ride.

Now, I choose to identify with the unmoving, unchanging space through which they are moving - grounded and present to life.

The space through which the movement occurs has become the most interesting thing.

The thing I personally was always looking for was true gnosis of the concepts I believed in, rather than the continual compromise of my mind mimicking the experience. The great blessing of the experience is alive, here in me. That is what my practice has given me - my own experience of this.

That is what is waiting for you too - your own experience. If that sounds far-fetched, let me ask you then to consider this...what would your experience of life be if you had just 10% more:

Ability to be PRESENT
PASSIONATE ALIVENESS
FOCUS + ENERGY
Consistent Spiritual CONNECTION
INNER PEACE
Sense of PURPOSE

You want the *embodied* awakening rather than the conceptualized awakening that leaves so many wanting.

As highlighted in my experiences above, you can have a lot more than 10%, but for you stubborn folks for whom capping it off seems more realistic, do sit with this notion.

Right now. What might life be like if it were your embodied reality?

Being Present is Coded Within Us

From this vantage point, I can see the utter genius in how everything is set up to serve our, and the collective, awakening.

I've now been witness to at least a thousand people in the quest of awakening. I've seen many stumble off, dazzled by endless seeking and dabbling out there.

I've seen far fewer badasses truly committed to the inner quest until the adventure is complete. I am not the only soul who came in to do this Ride or Die.

Even if you haven't identified as such up until this moment, meditation, being present, a badass state of consciousness - these are practices and you can cultivate this quality within you now.

If you have not yet completely found grace and purpose in your own karma, you are about to! You don't get to be in charge of how that all heals or manifests, but over time, with consistent practice, divine providence will make you a servant of embodied holy badassery too.

I have seen that the Universe has a built in code for us to return to that state of union from our birth. It has appeared that some of us came in with a clear burning desire to meet each quest required on this adventure and others not so much.

This is not a judgement. Statistics show 1% will follow-through all the way until it is done. I have to show up everyday like it's my job. And it is.

Now I wonder: which sort of Adventurer are you?

The Mythic Adventure into Badassery

Your Destiny isn't separate from you. It lies within you awaiting the right conditions to emerge through you.

Not everyone will bloom, just like not all seeds we attempt to sprout will do so. In fact, stats are quite low. 1%.

I'd love to see us change that status quo.

You can be part of that by taking action on what you come to know here and are encouraged to employ.

If you do not, anything I share about the possibility of waking up and cultivating a clear and consistent experience of the present moment isn't possible.

If you *do* take the actions, you will experience a life lived in the present moment, more and more. If you keep going and continue employing the suggestions made, you will live into higher states of consciousness - aka: "badassery."

Not all of you will do that. Some of you will just find a meditation practice - which is totally cool...and some of you won't even commit to that - which is also totally cool. It's good for you to know where you're at.

You may be here because you're anxious or you are looking for a stabilizing force. You may have felt that there is *something more*. You may have felt you are meant to do something bigger in this world.

You have likely tried several things. Some of it may have worked, some of it not. You may have tried to explore alone, within community, or through the guidance of a teacher.

Everyone will arrive here from their own unique set of circumstances. Each will get exactly what they are meant to. I am not attached.

Excepting to those of you who are tired of seeking and are ready to find a real relationship with the present moment. **You are who this book was written for.** You are who this work revolves around. You are why I exist. You are the ones humanity is waiting for - to recognize, stabilize, and serve in the embodied awakening of full human consciousness.

You are who I was told to watch for by the awakened masters on the planet, because you see, I am a "fisher of men" (and women). I am a spiritual midwife and I am answering your call.

You get to decide if you swim back into the sea of drones or come along for the most riveting adventure of any lifetime. As an ancient soul once said to me, "If you would go with me, who would stop you?" Very good question, grasshopper.

You need not ask anyone's permission, need not wait for any circumstances in your life to line up for you, need not fix or change anything about you or your life to be ready or worthy to come along.

Who would stop
you anyway, but a voice in your head trying to keep you comfortable in your endless seeking?

Are you ready to change your relationship with that voice and more importantly, with your eternal nature - your badass nature? If you know what I'm talking about, can I get a "hell yeah"!

Arriving to the Adventure

This is not a path, nor a task for the poser, safeguarding the conceptualization of a mindful, spiritual existence. This is a path and a task for you who are ready to devote yourself to the greatest love affair, mission and level of consciousness - those of you ready to passionately live your fundamental purpose.

I know you felt this knowing as a child. I know you knew you were here to do something important. I know that this knowing got smashed, hushed, made fun of, forgotten at the very least.

I know you got the impression that it isn't possible - except for the chosen few in some other millenia.

I know you've been searching and trying in various ways - and so you quietly, secretly feel this "just isn't your lot in this lifetime," or it would have worked out by now for you.

I know you don't even see the level of unconscious resolve to just accept this as your reality.

You can't see this belief that what has been is the way it is, because deep down, you are devastated or at least disappointed that you have not found embodied salvation, zest, and unbroken awareness of living your purpose every day.

But listen, Angel, it wasn't time yet.
And now this sacred quest is laid upon you.

Come forward to this razor's edge.
Together we will dance this non-linear path
of awakening and see this thing done until all
humans are awake.

I praise your courage to move toward that
bigness, that innocence and beauty, that joy
and passion. It can take great courage, grit,
devotion. That is no joke. But it is the only
way for the greatness in you to emerge and
be used up by the Universe.

If you do not come along on this adventure, I
won't judge you - you will lose no face.

Yet, join us and you won't be alone. I can hold
your hand.

You alone must do the inner work, however.
You alone are responsible to cultivate the
right conditions for you to level-up from
drone to awakened human.

You alone have to make the choice to shift
attention all day long - not just in meditation,
but in continuing to choose consciousness
over unconsciousness with eyes wide open.

You must bring your whole self and also be willing to let go of all you think you are as we proceed.

You are so very needed on this Adventure, for the whole of humanity. You would not be here otherwise. Make no mistake about that.

As an experienced adventurer, I can help guide. I have a map and know some of the terrain, monsters and other elements we will need to traverse.

When, a short way in you begin to doubt whether you really want this, to doubt you really are meant for this, to question whether you were delusional or just have better things to do, I'll be here adventuring on, reminding you, encouraging you, just as others have done and do for me.

If I'm not your cup of tea, there are others on the planet who could also hold your hand and guide you through these tricky Quests.

Find someone and stick with them for a time to see how this goes. Give yourself a real chance to no longer depend on conceptualization, analysis and the senses to determine how you are doing. Give yourself this gift and enjoy the aliveness, purpose, fulfillment and humble blessing of your own existence.

The 12th Hour

This is not time for messing around. At the time of this writing, there is a clear and contrasting percentage of people going deeper into fear, neurosis, addiction, depression, and divisiveness. There is an immense contrast which we can take advantage of right now - either life is scary, untrustworthy and unsafe - or it is magical, blessed, and perfect.

You have to choose which path you are going to be on. Which one sounds better? Neither is bad or wrong - one just sucks and one is incredibly beautiful.

I've been on both. One is a bad dream. The other is the only reality that ever was.

No one can take my word for this - prove me right or wrong - but go do the work to find out for yourself.

Reestablishing life in the present moment is easy. Meditation helps with this. Having an open eyes practice helps with this. Having qualified guidance is helpful with this.

I actually don't know any other way to do it. So that's why I'm here - to share some basic tools, tips and experience with you that you may begin to employ and implement as your new ritual - one that you prioritize above all others and at all cost.

At least for a time - until you've done enough research that you can say, 'Rodasi was full of shit.' Or more likely say, 'Holy cow she wasn't kidding!'

Guys, not many will follow through on the whole epic adventure. A lot of you *will* follow these initial instructions, however.

This means we together have the opportunity to bust some paradigms and status quo as you follow through into this conscious lifestyle of badassery - of life lived in the present moment.

Living Life Present is what we are supposed to be experiencing! It's super easy and super accessible so let's get started.

Taking on this Adventure, you are accepting responsibility as the shero or hero of your own life. You will meet the challenges of the many quests herein and notice how quickly the bold promises begin to come to fruition.

May the Force be with You.

A Sacred Pause

Walking the razor's edge of being awake to your life *is not always comfortable*.

But...there *is also* beauty and pleasure which *should be enjoyed*.

Om-ie, this journey is not only more enjoyable, but more effective when you are taking a playful approach!

I will continue to remind you to cultivate maximum enjoyment (as my spiritual teacher says).

So....let go of any heaviness and seriousness right now. Go on - shake it loose. Move. Breathe. Make some noise.
Vibe-up!

Karma to Dharma

Oh, Divine Creatrix of the manifest realm -
Essential Essence of Existence!

How cunning to instill in us seeds of
potential which can only be opened by the
great cosmic fires of the Holy Spirit.
These karmas we agreed to align with - so
that they might be useful in helping another
human trust enough to release separation,
returning to Your ultimate reality of Union.

How brilliant that everything in this manifest
realm says it is impossible - in particular the
initially elusive, hypnotizing thing called ego-
mind.
Making up the story of a separate self,
replaying it over and over in an attempt to
protect itself - lest it be revealed as illusory.
What bizarre and wondrous illusion this is!

Coming into this life with such apparent pain
and suffering, So much identification with
those comings and goings, lingering in the
muscles of the body and in the neural-
connections in the brain, making it all feel
and seem so REAL.

Oh the resistance of the mind, the body - out of fear of annihilation. Oh the cries of the world, "Don't drink the kool aid","What if you are wrong and you go to hell?," "Why can't you just be like everyone else?"

You built this passion and knowing in me so fiercely - setting everything up so perfectly for me to seek and find You. What remarkable trickery is this?

You were my true nature all along! Beloved, Your Grace swept through, healing the sense of separation - the illusion of the individual self. Began revealing this apparent karma as Your dharmic purpose.
You've shown me- the only reason I exist - to serve humanity in this same embodied realization! Great Creatrix of the Universe, I am in humble awe.
Jai Ma.

PART ONE

SHOWING UP TO THE
ADVENTURE OF BADASSERY

How to Approach this Adventure

"The price of anything is the amount of life you exchange for it." - Henry David Thoreau

"You can't cross the sea merely by standing and staring at the water." - Rabindranath Tagore

Keep It Real

I have been guilty of saying that I am *into* theater.

I can not tell you the last time I acted on stage or even went to watch live theater.

I have a friend who told me he's been involved in theater his whole life. I asked what he did last and when he'd be performing again. He told me he hadn't actually done anything since he was in high school. He is in his 40s.

He and I both have been believing a story that is not real.

People will tell me that they are "into" meditation, though they've never had a daily practice. Those of us who are actually into meditation do it currently, consistently, and typically several times every day, no matter what.

Where do you say you are into something, do something, or are a certain way, but it is not something you actually do in your real life?

Take a moment and consider this.

Did you do it?
Did you take that moment to consider?

If not, you might be one of the 99%.

There is a common life approach people take. I am still evolving out of said approach. It is an approach where we live in our head. We hear about something, memorize it, go deeper into our ability to understand and study it with our mind, gaining fancier more exact words to describe it.

We value this and call it intelligence.
We reward people for being smart and knowing things.

However, the truly successful, masterful people on the planet, in any given subject, actually live what they are studying and talking about.

How am I "evolving" out of this knowing vs living? By making conscious strides to actually live the practice of being present and not just feel righteous because I have heard what it is like.

This is like learning about the taste of chocolate rather than taking the chocolate into the mouth and discovering what the experience of chocolate is. I see this everywhere with most people, 99% of the time. It's our conditioning.

Unless, of course, I'm talking to my peers or mentors, or listening to my heroes and sheroes on the planet. Because those folks have taken a different approach to living.

These folks keep diving into each moment's experience, fully present, meeting life with great vigor and fervor.

These folks practice getting outside the comfort zone. They consistently lean into discomfort - into the unknown.

They do not fear failing as they don't see it as failing but rather as a point of sharpening the sword. These folks don't stop until they achieve what they are here to do.

Maybe you have and maybe you haven't been this sort of person. I never was. But I practiced and continue to practice and that is who I intend to be every day.

If that's of any interest to you, here's a suggestion:

Keep It Real. Implement everything you read in this guidebook! Don't just read. Play.

Exercises

How often do you live in the analytical, learning and thinking state of the mind?

You might be able to answer now, but sincerely, take half a day to watch and see.

Conversely, how much of your life do you live present to life with a quiet mind?

How much do you consciously prioritize, schedule, and otherwise put towards what you say you want?

How much energy do you give to peace of mind, evolution, happiness, consciousness?

How much time do you spend on self-care and spiritual practice currently?

It may be consistently several times a day, or it may be consistently not often.
Whatever is true for you, it is important to know what you are and are not doing.
Stop right now and consider this.
Journal about it.

Be open to seeing clearly.
This is essential for any degree of success here.

Sometimes we won't do this because we are afraid of what we know we will find. We keep choosing to ignore it. This is the state known as ignorance.

You can not transcend unless you look and see. Determine how you'd like to proceed with that honest information. Then apply a plan of action immediately and consistently in order to discover something new.

None of this self-examination is meant to be mean to yourself. None of it is meant to be a way of picking apart shortcomings - even though it could seem that way.

It is meant to breathe a pause into your life. It's meant to give you, for once, some space to stop and be with yourself.

When you do stop and just be with you, a whole lot of relief, beauty and goodness are revealed. Embrace it all so you can consciously proceed into a life of honest, clear awareness.

A life lived having replaced limiting beliefs and habits with consciousness and life-producing habits is heaven on earth.

And what is the best life-producing habit around? Being Present.

What's THE best tool creating that result? Meditation.

In this guidebook we embark on the badass adventure of replacing the old habits with the habit of being present to life. Together we learn how to lean into the now and truly live!

Structure of this Adventure

Let's set some structure up, Rockers!

One

Write down WHY you are doing any of this in the first place. Revisit your WHY when you fall off schedule, need to hit the reset button, or just every day to keep it fresh.

Consider the following:
- Why do you want to meditate?
- If you already meditate, why do you meditate?
- Why are you reading this book? What are you hoping the results will be? For example: are you wanting to go deeper? Why? Are you hoping to have a more consistent practice? Why? Are you looking

for a clear and consistent experience of peace? Why?

- Does a passionate life of badassery appeal to you? Why? What might that mean for you?
- What would be different in your inner and outer life if you were meditating, meditating more deeply, experiencing peace more consistently?
- What would be different in your inner and outer life if you felt in touch with your natural badassery - of being present a lot more consistently?

Two

Determine a timeframe that you will explore your journey of practicing meditation, being present and even getting this book read.

Write this commitment on your calendar for every one of the days you are commiting to.

Put it in your paper calendar or enter it into your electronic calendar - or both!

Do this now.

Three

Establish the habit of taking immediate action. The recommendation here is for you to begin to do so now.

Every time you read a suggestion, stop and do what is asked of you.

Four

You may notice that you need a reset on this immediate action-taking habit as well as on your commitment to practice.

Please keep this in mind and call yourself out when it happens. Then just hit the reset button.

Five

Add in daily Reminders to go off on your phone or computer, reminding you to: close your eyes, to be present, to read this book, to do the Questing exercises.

Schedule each of these activities in your planners now.

Prioritizing this Adventure through scheduling is important to set yourself up for success.

Six

Accountability is a critical element. This is why you are encouraged to engage in the **Rock Your Mind Global** Facebook group.

You may find other ways and forms of accountability. Please consider sharing your successes with us so we can benefit as well.

All of these points are important for you to succeed here. Prioritize them right now.

The Facebook Group

Go join the **Rock Your Mind Global** Facebook group.

Get it in your mind right now that you will interact in the FB group - because you are, at least for now, going to activate the excellence of the 1%ers and take action consistently for the period of time you've committed to.

- ☐ Introduce Yourself
- ☐ Share your WHY
- ☐ Share your personal commitment timeline and whatever else you'd like for us to witness.

It would be normal to feel a little nervous or unsure to do the above, but you must. It will help you snap out of some old habits and forge some much better ones - all of which will serve you in becoming better able to be present.

If you aren't willing to, that's an old habit of a lackluster life and we are replacing that habit with badassery, right? So...go do it.

It's important that you publicly express your why. Doing so may make your ego-mind squirm, but it will move you into a new level of badassery immediately.

Any discomfort should be identified as an old habit dying - being burnt up by Shakti (the Holy Spirit).

Claiming your place in the global Facebook group also allows the Universe (and all of us) to see that you are serious and it will line up to support you.

We all help hold one another accountable when diversion happens, compromise is engaged, or the heat gets turned up. We are in this together and need one another for this to work.

Quest Goals

Quest Goals are what you will be encouraged to take action on throughout the badass adventure of reading this guidebook.

Quest Goals will help you in establishing your meditation and consciousness lifestyle.

You will find most of these Quest Goals at the end of each chapter, but a few will be strewn throughout the text.

Now that you understand Quest Goals and you've scheduled time for reading, practice and engagement, please bear in mind that consistency every day is required to anchor a habit.

Rock and Roll, People! Let's Continue!!!

Best Practices for Badassery

The secret of change is to focus all of your energy not on fighting the old, but on building the new. - Socrates

These best practice suggestions are for you to achieve maximum success as you develop proficiency in skill, gain expertise, and continuously level-up into new ranges of possibility.
Enjoy!

• Have an open mind. If you find you are arguing with me about what I am saying is possible, or about how some quest isn't going to work for you, stop and breathe and consider "what if I can have that experience? What if I *can* find success in that Quest somehow?"

Just as importantly - if you find yourself agreeing with me, stop and breathe and do the questing homeworks - because it's just as limiting to stop yourself from agreeing in the mind as it is to disagree in the mind.

Both happen in the mind, but neither are doing the questing homework.
Read this again.

- Consider: what may keep you from actually doing your practice? Be honest with yourself and prepare to pull up those bootstraps when you see those moments show up. Name those special circumstances - and make a plan to do it anyway. Let us know what these are and let us know when you break through so we can celebrate with you!

- Close eyes in Meditation at least once a day, for 20 minutes.

- When and where will you practice? Decide now.

- Practice open eyes exercises of coming present at least 3 times a day.

- Who is your accountability partner/team - your tribe of adventurers? Let your family or housemates, your workmates, the people in your life know what you are up to and set the boundary to not be distrubed during this sacred time. (Do not skip this step - it is a must.)

- When are you engaging in the Rock Your Mind Global Facebook group? Schedule it.

- Do the Quest homework right away and post about it right away - all in the same day. This is a great habit to get into and ensures you get the most out of this experiential journey.

- Remember your WHY and let us know when you are slacking - set yourself up for success and continue to recalibrate as needed forever! Let that be a game - see how you can be playful!

- Start a Meditation for Badassery book club live or virtual. Get a few other folks to join you in this adventure! When you do so, share with us how it's going.

Your spiritual armor is achieved in these above ways. You exercise the muscles of the 1% in these ways. You replace the old habits with the new in employing these practices. Badassery unfolds in this way.

What is more important than this?

Please recognize...
You've been taught that *everything* is more important. The world values worldly things. We are reversing that habit and belief.

This is the most important thing. Everything else in life is blessed as a result of prioritizing this. Investigate and find out for yourself.

This book is not meant to be 'shelf-help' for you, but to support you in an experiential cosmic adventure into superhuman badassery.

So who do you want to be in the adventure of your own life?

a)   One who wakes up to a zesty badass life truly serving others

OR

b)   One who lets a voice in your head win - derailing you into the lackluster delusion of the drone state, endlessly trying to improve and never finding what you are looking for.

A Map Key for this Badass Adventure

In each chapter you will find Poems, Quotes, Exercises, Key Points, and the Quest Goals.

You will also find suggestions, including going to my website, signing up for Insight Timer, engaging in the Facebook group, closing your eyes.

Poems

The poems are my love affair with the divine. They are my experience of practicing meditation and of evolving consciousness. Poetry is not meant to be understood - but to point at an experience.

Poetry transmits a vibration. Read them resting back inside of yourself and see what vibration remains.

Quotes

When you read the quotes, really be present. Stop and drink it in. Don't analyze it. See what experience it is transmitting for you. Be with the quote. Let it into your bones. Then proceed to read the chapter.

Exercises

You will come across Exercises as you read. Some will be practice Exercises and some will be Contemplative Exercises.

Take time out to actually do these as you come across them!

Suggestions + Quest Goals

Anytime you come across a suggestion, within the text or in the Questing Goals sections, stop immediately and apply what you've been offered.

See what happens as a result of employing the suggestion, but also, notice that in taking immediate action, you are changing your relationship to life, consciousness, and adventure.

Key Points

The same goes for key points - be present, see if it is your experience, see if it makes sense, see if you got something different from the chapter.

A Good Formula to Follow

Stay alert to each new moment as you read and employ these practices.
Keep coming back to the moment with all of your attention. Use the act of reading this book and employing these practices as the practice of being present!

Here's what would be super cool for you to squeeze the absolute most out of this investment: **_give it your all._**

Be willing to be adventurous. Be curious - stay alert to what happens as you do so.

And when all else fails, please get up and shake your booty or bang your head to some great music you love. Laugh really loudly. Play. Fun is also a requirement. Got it? Good.

- Make a sincere commitment. Make it Non-negotiable.

- Make that commitment public and get some buddies (new or current) to join you.

- Have a playful attitude, an open-mind, and be curious. When you notice that you are not, when you are taking it seriously and not able to snap out of it - get some help.

- Sit down at least 20 minutes each day. If you already have a steady daily practice, do 2-3 times a day for at least 20 min each time. For example: before breakfast, before dinner, before bed.

- Use effective meditative and consciousness tools to use with eyes closed and open.

- Get competent and experienced guidance to help you go through pitfalls - beyond the subtle tricks of the mind. Continue deepening, expanding and stabilizing real growth into said higher states.

- Design your life around your practice. Alert the people in your life that you won't be available during these times.

- Keep sharing your experiences with your teacher or those who've gone before you to keep getting support and guidance.

- Add in a deeper dive. This may look like a weekend event, a weeklong retreat or some kind of immersive training.

- Expect you'll have to reset and recommit. Expect that it will appear that you are "going backwards." Expect this and prepare for it. Hit the reset button and get going again.

Common Pitfalls

- Don't complicate it. Don't be lazy. Keep it simple, but stay devoted.

- Thoughts are a natural part of life and meditation - decide now that you don't care if you have them.

- Emotions are a part of life. Decide now that you won't let them overcome you, but you won't push them away either. Instead, you will make your practice more important than your emotions.

- Don't be arrogant and don't decide you already know what to expect. Continue being curious and gentle and attentive to what is right now.

- Set yourself up for success but expect diversions. Exercising the muscle requires diversion. Who cares if you become diverted?

Self-judgment takes a lot of energy. It's a waste. We get to strengthen the muscle of being present when we come back from a diversion. So celebrate and keep going.

KeyPoints

★   You are sovereign hero or shero of this adventure; you are solely responsible for the outcome based on your devotion to doing the work

★   You are not alone. We are in solidarity - all of us committed to this path of awakening, and some of us adventurers are gathered under this little umbrella, as part of this tribe for maximum enjoyment and effectiveness

★   Your destined awakened, up-leveled self is only going to emerge if you really engage in this Adventure and do the Questing work

★   The world is waiting for you to awaken to full human consciousness so that it can rise and celebrate too

Quest Goals

★   Let the people in your life know that you are embarking on this adventure into meditation and that you are learning how to be present. Let them know that you need their support - in your home, at work, with your friends, on social media.

 Let them all know so that you can protect your sacred space to succeed at this adventure and maybe gain some fellow adventurers close to you at the same time.

★   Get accountability partner and schedule check-ins with them

★   Visit RodasiCampbell.com for more resources.

★   Use hashtags like: #21daymeditationjourney #rockyourmind #meditationforbadassery #rodasicampbell on social media to share the LOVE!

PART TWO

CONSCIOUSNESS MINDSET

In The Beginning We Knew Badassery

"Tell me, what is it you plan to do with your one wild and precious life?"
- Mary Oliver

Life begins in innocence.
Life begins with us swimming in fascination, flow, in oneness. Life begins with attention effortlessly resting inward.

Science suggests that our sympathetic and parasympathetic nervous systems are in balance and harmony in our early childhood (unless there is prenatal or birth trauma).

Things are good. Oxytocin pours in as we are held close to the bodies of those who care for us, as other humans look us in the eye and hold our gaze. We experience the magic and wonder of life.

Do you remember?

When first asked this myself two decades ago, all I could remember was the tough stuff - and there was a lot of it.

But given a few more moments of sitting still, I began to recall the magic and wonder of the plants - the hollyhocks, chicory, wild strawberry and cedar trees. I remember knowing I could talk to the animals and control the elements.

I knew love, connection and aliveness. There was pure magic and flow.

Ancient history + prophecy suggest that this cycle of unconsciousness, the appearance of the evolution of consciousness and the destiny of humanity to awaken is prophesied, calculated, pre-determined, destined - right on time.

We "fall asleep" for a reason. For thousands of years very few discover the point and "wake" while still alive. This is changing.

Why I Think You Are Here

Don't die without embracing the daring adventure your life was meant to be.
- Steve Pavlina

Consider the cover of this book.

Meditation and Conscious Awakening are way less glamorous than the cover as are most of our collective erroneous ideas about these things.

But the inner experience of life, as a result of a consistent movement toward awakening, can be very much like the essence of the cover.

The aliveness and passion, the happiness and connection you may recognize in the cover image, I attribute to my commitment to conscious evolution and to my meditative practice.

This is a state which emerges and takes root as a result of such a devotion to being present to life. You were drawn to that state. It is a radiance you know inside of you and you want to rest in that more fully and more consistently.

That's why you are here.

It's not me. Not Marketing. It is the transmission of this state having been received and recognized in you. That says a lot about you.

This radiance humbly comes to anyone with practice. Meditation dissolves stress, rewires the brain, changes the chemical soup, focuses the mind, and gives space for the Universe's radiance to pour forth.

That's what happens when we meditate. We get cleaned out. Like a cosmic pipe cleaner, people. Literally.

You want that. You want to be cleaned out and rewired.

You deeply yearn to be a steady, sure vessel for the radiance of your own presence to shine forth. AND...You gonna get you some of that, Om-ie.

Meditation has freed me from debilitating anxiety, depression, addictions, fearful thoughts and actions. Meditation has replaced the habits of seeking endlessly in my mind, unconsciously avoiding truly living life, with new habits of showing up awake and present to life.

Sometimes it can present as blissful, nurturing, approachable and comforting. Other times, it can present as unwaveringly still - and that can really freak the ego out.

I love the freedom and effortlessness of keeping present and watching life unfold - rather than the old way of trying to control, force and judge. Trying to be. Trying to fit. Trying to heal. Trying to figure it all out.

Do you know what that's like - being the controller of the Universe?

Lordy, is that ever exhausting!
If you know what I mean, it's time to retire from that job, isn't it?
Hell. yeah.

You want this kind of freedom to be whatever the Universe calls you to be. You want to know the passionate aliveness and the ease within a state of holy surrender.

You exist to experience the level of reality that you were born into: a state of oneness. A state where love, peace, and happiness are unconditionally present.

You, cosmic adventurer, exist to be aware of, tuned to, and transmitting the aliveness of this state. In this state there is humble appreciation of just existing. Not fabricated moods. A state. Of consciousness.

In taking on such an Adventure, you find freedom from the limiting, drone-ish existence. You've been seeking relief from this state in a myriad of ways.

With practice here, that state of consciousness is replaced with one of riveting aliveness. A state of vast inner silence. An experience so rich and full, infinite, and all-consuming that you find it humorous that you could have ever been asleep enough to not notice it's been here all this time.

You came here to bring in certain karma. In waking up to the present moment, you realize these karmas as your spiritual purpose. Those karmas were never meant to be the end-all nor just your lot in life.

That perception is from the waking state of the average human. Those perceived limitations you've been inside of led you here right?

That's so cool. Thank God for that.

You are here in these pages because you are already waking and remembering. There is a call in all of consciousness, in all humans, to return to that inner silence and become engaged in the most epic, badass love affair that has or ever will exist.

You are answering that call right now.

Likely you've already been doing some things to improve yourself and your life. Maybe even for decades.

You are ready now to go from seeking and hitting glass ceilings, to truly finding. You are ready to find the thing that you couldn't quite put your finger on, but has been summoning you in its elusiveness.

I'm very excited about that. Because you're gonna find it, baby. It truly has been "seeking" you. You just had the wrong map and wrong directions.

And now you have this book. It's like a portkey. You choose what you do herein, but it's the right map and right directions. It'll show you the way and beyond if you let it.

Are you stoked yet? OMG!

You won't escape your destiny to wake up in this lifetime now that you've held the portkey.

That is, unless you abandon your mythic adventure and do not accept the Questing it asks of you.

Traversing Evolution

Evolution is happening.
There's a way evolution happens slowly and unconsciously, and there is a way it happens faster and consciously.

Unfortunately there are many people who think that they are conscious because they have identified themselves as such. They live their lives in certain ways that the mind has determined as conscious.

From a higher vantage point this is adding color to a puff of smoke. The puff of smoke remains a puff of smoke.

Common States of the Average Human

1)   Ignorance with zero desire to wake up
2)   Desire while being identified as already "woke"
3)   Exploring the experience of embodying higher states of consciousness, but stopping at a taste. Again identified with already "knowing".

None of the above is actively being in a measurable state of higher consciousness.

Humbly Beyond the *Common*

Another option is to embody a higher state of consciousness. That is a true evolution.

In this experience the puff of smoke is seen through for what it is. Before there was an intoxicating notion of being *spiritual* within a hypnotic dream.

Now there is a substantial living experience of the cosmic container inside of which the smoke appears.

Without guidance I wouldn't have known there was a difference, nor would I have ever been able to tell that difference inside of me.

I could see a difference in those I admired. I could feel it. I didn't know what that thing was, but I knew I wanted it.

One of the biggest traps is that the mind can mimic the experience and believes it is having the experience when it is not. It was only with keen guidance that I could begin to discern the mimicking ego from true embodiment.

This remains my Quest.

We all start inside that puff of smoke though. That's of course where I was at before finding the tools and support to help me begin to traverse the very wild adventure of conscious evolution.

Truth is, in the moments that I slip briefly back into unconsciousness, I am right back inside that smoky dream. The difference is that wakefulness is my new setpoint and awareness returns back to resting in presence quickly.

It is exquisite to see the contrast. What a beguiling and bewitching thing the mind is!

Honestly, it was devastating and terrifying to discover that spiritual concept and the voice of the "wise" spiritual ego - had to be surrendered in order to actually evolve.

For years I relied upon that voice as my awakened self, yet I was in great error.

I saw an unmitigated fear that without the conceptualization, without mental tracking of apparent spiritual growth, evolution would not take place. Ironically, this is the exact opposite of the truth.

Conceptualization makes a prettier and endless puff of smoke. Surrendering that mental movement clears the smoke immediately, revealing still, silent presence.

I'm also excited to share that this whole issue was quickly far less interesting than the continual discovering of said presence. I did and do require the continual assurance of my teacher that I'd be ok and better off without this dependence.

Rite of Passage

The difference between these two states is HUGE. In fact spiritual-concept dependence is universes away from the actual state of being truly present.

Assume that unless you have a super clear and unwavering experience of the present moment with zero mental chatter, you have habits to be surrendered. Including ones you cherish and will not like having to let go of.

> **Luke: "I'm not afraid."**
> **Yoda: "You will be. You will be."**
> ***Empire Strikes Back***

This is an important point in everyone's evolution. No one skips over it or just doesn't have it happen. Virtually no one in history has ever achieved this without immersive support from one who has gone before on the path of consciousness. This is what Teachers are for.

If you have not yet had the pleasure of facing the terror, horror, embarrassment and shock come upon you, the only reason why is that you have not yet come present enough for long enough.

This is one signpost determining that you might not be "woke" just yet.
Just keeping it real here, folks.
That's a requirement of badassery.

Stick around and play and you will come to this point. When you do, I will celebrate with you. Even while you are trying not to be afraid or trying not to judge yourself. You'll have a hand to hold through these moments, if you are willing.

The Emerging State of Badassery

There is a paradox in this Adventure. One that will dissolve over time. It appears to be a paradox I should say. Because it actually isn't. You are perfect now, and evolution is happening.

You are already whole and complete. Your pure presence is already perfectly badass. You may not see or feel this. Or maybe you claim it, yet still wonder why it's not sustainable to your bones.

I once liked this concept of wholeness, but was very confused about how to get my own stable experience of it until I was led by my own teacher.

There were also times that like wholeness and oneness angered me or made me gag. That's because I deeply believed that they were b.s. or underneath of that, I believed these realities to be out of my reach.

I was wrong about both. I just needed proper instruction and support. I was too in my head spiritually and did not know how to get out without help.

I had a habit of being attentive to and identified with the movement of the mind, the way the body felt and the circumstances of life. Some people call that being mindful.

However, it is an erroneous view. This kind of life focus creates the delusion of separation and the belief in the need to go get the thing we lack and need.

Since we so completely believe this we and the Universe create those congruent conditions which support and make this state seem very real.

Until that habit is seen and the clear habit of resting inward, identified as pure presence is consciously engaged to replace it, then you will be unable to embody this truth.

You will, scientifically speaking, remain asleep in drone-mode and always have a niggling feeling that there is something more outside your reach - no matter how hard you try to do all the right things to evolve. Maybe you see this as your own experience now.

Until one is super clear, doubt and reliance on mind remain. The mind can never show the way.

For me, a teacher who went through the journey into badassery has been essential. The landmines of the mind and the attraction to life's compulsions are absolutely insidious. Without help, it is near impossible to transcend.

Some Science on Being Badass

Yet transcendence is our birthright.
The code of superhuman badassery is in us.
That code is unlocked in you to varying degrees and that is why you are here.

We must cultivate the right conditions through practice and playful engagement throughout our days to re-establish life in the present moment. This becomes our set-point. This becomes our M.O.

The state of resting attention within is highlighted in ancient spiritual cultures around the world: Turya, Samadhi, Satori, the peace that passeth understanding. This fourth state is one where we are mentally alert but know a quiet peace.

The body is exhibiting a much different chemical soup than that in the typical waking state human - far less stress hormones, far more happy hormones, and other physiological markers which are measurable.

For example, an EEG machine would document brain coherence. By attaching leads to the left and right hemispheres of the brain on the parietal, occipital and temporal lobes, we can measure that brain waves are quite chaotic in the typical human experience.

When someone is meditating or when someone is being present, the surface cortex becomes coherent. This is a measurement of inner peace. To objectively rest inward while subjectively experiencing this peace is our natural state.

We were just never taught how to cultivate it. This cultivation leads to an anchoring of this state.

What we focus on and what we practice becomes our mode of operation, it becomes memorized, it becomes hard-wired.

There is an analogy my lineage uses in teaching new students that speaks to this stabilization. In olden times, and still with dye-artisans, cloth was dipped into dye and then left in the sun to fade.

The cloth was dipped into the dye again. Left to fade in the sun again. This time, it doesn't fade as much. Dip again, fade again. The color becomes both color-fast as well as brighter or deeper. It becomes permanent.

The analogy speaks to how exercising this muscle certainly leads to this stability of the fourth state.

We benefit from understanding both that it is guaranteed if we keep going and that what appears to be "going backwards" is an important part of the whole deal and should be welcomed as such.

We practice meditation and being present with eyes open, like dipping into dye.

Attention goes outward into the senses, thoughts, emotions and circumstances, like the sun fading the dye. In this way attention leaves the present moment, moving outward.

Out of habit attention leaves awareness of the still, silent presence within. It then returns to alertness of the now, immersing back into the cosmic dye.

Recognize the import of contrast. Expanding consciousness and the contraction back to the old habit is wild and beautiful. The appearance of forgetting and going unconscious again is an important part of how we stabilize.

This is a joyful cosmic flow, though in initial awareness of this, one may work through some habits of judgment and frustration.

We assist the familiarity and ultimate stabilization by getting our eyes closed and consciously choosing to return. We assist by consciously choosing with our eyes open, employing whatever tools.

At some point, in a sense, no tools are needed as we become so familiar with this state. Like being in the stressed out waking state was our previous setpoint, our new setpoint has become being present.

On the way to this stabilized state, we become clear about how to immediately rest back inward. Bam. Done. Doesn't that sound awesome? It's doable too.

KeyPoints

★   Life began in an awakened state.

★   We can return to that state.

★ The return is guaranteed with the use of right tools, support,and consistent cultivation of congruent conditions.

★ States of Consciousness are measurable by Science.

★ Gaining intellectual, spiritual knowledge is not at all the same thing as embodying spiritual principles.

★ We've been taught to learn and celebrated for our intellect.

★ Awakening requires the courage to relinquish our habituated dependence on the mind, and to live into embodiment.

★ This is not comfortable in the beginning, but it is very simple.

★ Over time being present becomes your setpoint rather than being a stress-filled drone.

★ Over time life becomes rivetingly alive and fluid rather than the initial discomfort. We habituate leaning into the edge of right now. Rather than fear, we feel the rightness of being so awake to right now.

Quest Goals

★   Sit in meditation for 20 minutes at least once today. If you already have a solid meditation practice, make it twice a day or sit once for a longer period. For example add 10 minute increments over time.

★   Remind yourself to come very present at least 3 times today. If you've already been playing with silencing your mind and coming very present with eyes open - including with the use of Mantra, Mindfulness, Nature as tools, then take your personal practice to a new level for you.

★   Do a little research on the Science behind Meditation and being present - how it impacts the brain and the nervous system.

★   Take note of how life is unfolding as a result of practicing. Do you feel more connected and on-point already? Are things already getting brighter and more fluid?

Or - maybe you are being forced to look at what is not working in your thoughts, feelings, behaviors or relationships - maybe you are becoming more aware.

That won't feel comfortable, but it is an awesome sign of healing and growth. Share it with us in the **Rock Your Mind Global** Facebook group, friend.

We Exist to Follow the Bliss

God, I always felt a deep need to understand why I exist - why life exists.
That desire was inspired by the perception of pain. You gave me such a fire to know!
I could not stop no matter what else came in front of me.
There were times that I listened to the voices of those around me, hoping I would stop seeking and just settle comfortably alongside them. Sometimes I would try, but invariably You brought me back.
This was what the heart wanted more than anything and could not stop. I had to give everything to it.
So patiently, unconditionally and consistently did You give me chance after chance to surrender to this deepest, truest desire.

No matter how afraid along the journey I
have been, You have gifted me with the
ultimate comfort in You.
Through practice, through the guidance of a
Teacher, through nature, through any means
possible.
If I had but the eyes to see it this way.
You cleared the cobwebs from these eyes
and continue to strengthen the ability to see

Your light and grace in everything always.
You have revealed this as my bliss and my
purpose and my deep desire fulfilling itself.

After such delusion of separation and pain,
You have granted me awareness that my
home in heaven with You is in each cell of
this body, of this universe, and in the stillest
part of awareness, unmoving, unchanging,
eternal, union.
Jai Ma.

The Game of Consciousness

"Your duty is to be; and not to be this or that. 'I am that I am' sums up the whole truth. The method is summed up in the words 'Be still'... Give up the notion that 'I am so and so'." - Sri Ramana Maharishi

Looking for love in all the wrong places.
Looking for _____ in all the wrong places.
That is what we've been taught to do.
Seek outside of ourselves for all of the fundamental needs.

What bizarre insanity, when what we've been seeking has been here within us all along.

For example, we've all been taught that it is important to our worth in this world that we be successful. We have been taught that success will bring us something to be proud of and worthy of and it will provide us with happiness.

We have been taught that success has to do with our level of abundance in the form of wealth. We have been taught that wealth is attained when we have a certain amount of money, things, and status.

All of this is dependent on outside circumstances. Let's explore this.

Exercise

Sit comfortably.
Keep your eyes open.
Simply begin to notice all that is in front of you.
Let your awareness be wide.
Drink in the environment surrounding you.

If you're having a difficult time allowing for yourself to really imbibe in what is surrounding you, close your eyes for a few moments.

Following the breath or using your mantra, drop in and get present.

Once you're able to feel connected and present, begin to look around your environment again.

Notice the abundance that surrounds you. Notice the abundance of spaciousness and the abundance of gravity.

If you have access to nature, even if it's outside the window, observe and consider the abundance of air, of earth, of trees, plants, animals and humans.

Notice the abundance of that which is surrounding you in this life - in this Universe.

Now close your eyes, again dropping deeply into the center of yourself.
Rest back.

Nowhere to go, nothing to do, nothing to understand or achieve.

Notice the abundance of life within your body. Notice the blood and fluid moving through your body. Consider the abundance of spaciousness inside of each atom - 99.9% spaciousness.

Notice the intelligence that allows for your organs, tissues and body systems. Notice how this flow of life force contributes to the functions of your body - the abundance of being alive.

Notice the abundance of creative intelligence.

Sit with the abundance that you have access to inside the body and outside the body.

Now let your awareness go to the edges of the Universe.

Explore the sense of abundance, the vastness of consciousness available. Notice the infinite number of things that exist within the Universe.

Notice how you've tuned into the frequency and reality of abundance.

Bring awareness back to the body.
Feel the felt sense of being held by gravity.

Take a deep breath, exhaling naturally.

Allow your attention to come to your surroundings.

Slowly open your eyes, noticing the abundance that is remaining here for you. Be Still. Be alert.

Consider what success, happiness and abundance might actually look like were we not bound by conditioning.

Would you like to put a stake in the ground for this new paradigm of success, happiness and abundance?

If you find that your heart pulls you forward into this paradigm, it is recommended that you play with this abundance practice as often as you can remember until it becomes a new setpoint for you.

The Wrong Map

You got some bad information from the time you were a kid just like the rest of us.

We were all taught to seek love, peace of mind, validation, accolades, praise, our worth - everything outside of us. I don't know how we screwed that up, man.

Jesus said "seek ye first the kingdom of heaven," and he also said that the kingdom of heaven is within. He did not say seek love, peace, God, wholeness - outside of you and then you'll get the kingdom of heaven. Seems pretty clear to me.

Somewhere we came to believe in the wrong map. This map's directions have crippled us. It has taught us that we are our thoughts, emotions, and body. That our circumstances dictate our level of internal freedom.

The current map shows us how to improve a dream that we are witness to, but that is not what or who we are. Like a dreamer lost in a dream, we believe it is real and that this is all that there is.

Being identified with the limited "me" that the mind has created, we suffer. We are plugged into the wrong reality. In fact, we are not plugged in to reality at all - this is why we suffer. The wrong map has us move attention outward and in mental analysis.

The wrong map has us bound to mental conceptualization and identified with a limited, mistaken identity- one that may likely not even exist.

Humans live lives that are not at all in the present moment - playing out illusory storylines until the body dies.

How shocking it must be to drop the body in death and find out we had it all wrong the entire time. An entire life wasted in a dream.

The Tree of Life

The root stress of our modern world is a sense that there is *something wrong*. Since we are habituated to seek outside ourselves we look around trying to figure out how to fix life and ourselves to make that sense go away.

With the right instruction, we find this sense that *something is wrong* exists because our attention is in the wrong place.

We aren't following Jesus's instructions (or any other Sage from history). We are doing the exact opposite.

You see, we feel there is something wrong, because we are brilliant. We innately know we are meant to be resting attention inward - that this is where and how we feel on-purpose, connected, alive, free.

We intuitively know that this is how we heal the *sense* that there is *something wrong* and how we come to have *all else added unto* us.

The moment that I saw this clearly for myself it became seared into my mind.

I was talking to a fella at the meditation community and training facility where I lived in 2000. He was reflecting something he saw in me which was uncomfortable - because it was true.

My go-to reaction around that subject matter would have been to become defensive and shut it down, as if I were receiving criticism or an attack. Instead, I saw with new eyes. I was in awe of the underlying sense that there was something wrong with me.

Further, I could see that I was being gifted with awareness and love. Mind blown.

It was like all the moments in my life where this had ever occurred, with this subject matter or otherwise, was culminating right here. I was somehow awake enough to recognize that it had always been a gift of love.

I realized I had simply been unable to experience it that way with the built up stress in my nervous system, the wiring of my brain and the erroneous beliefs I held.

Where a longstanding concept of "everything is God's love coming at us" deepened into my own experience - I was set free to see this underlying defense mechanism everywhere in my life.

Sincere compassion rose within me along with the capacity to change my relationship to this thing. That exploration continues today.

In this wrong map approach we try to heal and change ourselves by watering or hacking off the limbs of the tree of life rather than going to the foundational root of it.

We spend immense amounts of time, energy and money on fixing ourselves and our lives - focused on the problem.

When we deepen into an embodied relationship with the still, silent part of ourselves, and with the present moment, it is obvious that we can only heal (aka awaken) upon approach of the root.

We give attention to the solution, to the source of solutions - and in doing so we begin to rewire, recalibrate, see where we can stop trying to fix the limbs, and give everything to nourishing the root.

In the wrong map approach we think we have tons of things to do in order to be *right enough* to know peace, purpose, success. In the *right map* approach we know that there is one thing to do first and all else is presented clearly from there.

You must see this strange hypnotism for yourself. You have to see it in action in your life - not just comprehend what I am saying. When you do, it will *rock your foundation*.

In order to *break on through to the other side* - like Neo in The Matrix, it must be rocked. So much of what you think you know about yourself and about existence is either a small, partial, limited truth or it is a complete delusion. The right map will rectify this for you in the most beautiful, joyous way.

The goal of the wrong map is to seek everything out there - because out there is where everything is.

We also are taught that if we work hard to get all the things that will make us happy, then we will earn a right to rest and find peace in retirement. How is that plan working for us?

This leads so many folks to have the sense that they just don't have time and can not risk taking time for peace right now.

Now we are going to be curious - and this is imperative, people - how much of your day, your thoughts, your actions, your life is about this wrong map? Stop and notice.

KeyPoints

★ We have had the wrong map. It leads us outward, endlessly seeking. This never fulfills the true inner needs.

★ The right map leads us inward - to be still.

★ Don't tend the branches of the Tree of Life. Tend the Root.

★ This is when and how the joyful consciousness reveals itself and we awaken from the delusion of separation from what we seek.

Quest Goals

★ Consider the wrong map and how it has manifested in your life.

★ Consider the Tree of Life analogy. Can you see how you have watered the tree branches instead of the Root?

★ Consider the right map and how watering the root of the Tree of Life would manifest different results in your life.

★ If you feel so called, share what you discover in the **Rock Your Mind Global** Facebook group.

Cosmic Play

I forever turned outward searching for Your presence.
Without understanding what I was looking for, or how I'd know that I'd found You when I had. I was lost; bewildered in a dream of endless seeking and suffering.
A thousand explosions of initial shock, momentary embarrassment and finally immense relief to discover You've been here in every corner, smile, taste, breathe.
You've always rested here within as the very presence that is witness to this life.
You, the one true and ultimate beloved.
What a strange game of hide-and-seek this was.
One where I was hypnotized by the dance of consciousness, enamoured, drunk with the erroneous messages that it gave me - that You and anything important were out there somewhere.
When all along, the veil had just come down hiding Your presence, Love's presence from me. What joy - to discover that I was never severed from Your loving pipeline of goodness, holiness, purpose, consciousness. I

know today I could not be alive were that the case.

You have animated every part of this existence.

I am humbled to have believed I was ever lost, ever separate, ever unworthy - when all along, there was the simple yet profound and today obvious fact, that this existence was always Yours.

The pain was not in the things which befell me or around me or because of me.

The pain existed because of the erroneous belief that I had to seek outside of myself for You, for the fundamental, for myself.

That pain was telling me that something was wrong alright - I had the wrong set of instructions, bewitched in a lie. It felt sinister and maleficent.

As You continue to awake in this heart, every bit of it has been on purpose, on point, right on time and in holy order.

Hell was in the forgetting, the illusion of separation, the appearance of a journey toward you with the wrong map all along.

That hell, once woken from, has filled me with such delight.

What a wild game of hide-and-seek.

Thank you, Eternal One.

Jai Ma.

Principles of Badassery

"Whatever we put our attention on will grow stronger in our life."
- Maharishi Mahesh Yogi

"Life is meant to be lived in Eternal Joy, Infinite Freedom, Unbounded Awareness. Any other life is utterly missing the point of being born a human." - MSI

Some key principles must now be looked at to help get your mindset right for badassery. These are Universal spiritual principles.

Hopefully I've done enough clear marketing to attract the folks who are down with this. You may, however, be brand new to this type of thing.

Either way, I invite innocence, curiosity, open-mindedness. I invite in the willingness to *feel-into*, not just think about and analyze what is being offered below.

In fact, it will be of great use for the rest of life to drop into experience, rather than intellectualize meaning (as we've all been taught to habituate).
Right on. Let's proceed...

With proper perspective you are more likely to succeed at cultivating congruent conditions for the maintenance of higher states of consciousness.

Personal + Professional Development gurus say that mindset is 80% of our driving force. It determines whether we succeed or fail. The other 20% is right action.

Principle One

Everything is happening for you - not to you. Do not assume you know what this means. Do not assume you have mastered this. (the gods would laugh)

Look to see where you can get into the practice of being present and curious -

especially in moments of challenge, discomfort and intensity.
Guaranteed your mind is at least unconsciously believing you are a victim. The shift can be swift, but you must actually make the shift - not just think about making it.

Principle Two

Nothing is yours so you might as well practice treating your life as borrowed, precious, rare and amazing.

The body, the mind, the conditioning, the desires, feelings, awarenesses, the growth, the relationships, the things you 'own,' the money, the investments, the businesses - none of it is yours. You are a steward of it.

What will you do with this "one wild and precious life", beloved: Drone it out, or Rock it out?

Principle Three

The Universe exists to serve you. It *does* have your back. You may not be in energetic alignment with that yet, but meditation and consciousness practices will fix that for you.

Understand this and be open to it revealing itself to you as a living experience.

You are supported and loved. You've never been separate from the thing that created you (not talking about the sperm and egg stuff here).

Consciously engage and co-create with this universal life force energy, or God if you will.

Principle Four

You are not here to suffer. It is an option. It is a choice. That choice lies in accepting the challenges and pain as amazing creations of the universe unfurling before your eyes - inside or outside.

Shift focus to this being a life of amazement and awe, of badassery and wonder.

You were not meant to come here and struggle and just barely survive - nor were you meant to externally thrive while being spiritually bankrupt.

Some folks are doing alright, feeling pretty good about the inside and outside. That is great, contentment is beautiful. And a little more alertness and devotion to walking the razor's edge of aliveness and practicing contentment here is *badass*.

Principle Five

Being Awake is Your Abundant Birthright. Unbounded Awareness, Infinite Possibility, Great Joy - is your birthright.

The 4th state and beyond is your birthright. It's not just for a chosen few. It's for you.

You are meant to be superhuman ninja jedi. You are meant to live with vitality, curiosity, connection, purpose, and peace. You are meant to deeply understand why you exist and what you are here to do.

Principle Six

What you focus on is amplified.

Quantum physics notes that what is being focused upon is affected by the observer. The Law of Attraction tells us that our vibration affects that which we create in our lives. Henry Ford said something like, "Whether you think you can or you can't, either way you are right."

If you focus on your issues, even if it's trying to fix and heal them, your focus is "issues". And that is what you're going to experience.

If you focus on and cultivate the states of praise, peace, gratitude, love, generosity, compassion, then that is what you will know in your experience.

Just do a little research in your own life on this and you'll see that what you focus on is amplified.

You can take an honest assessment of who you seem to be and how you are and are not showing up in the world without dramatic embellishments of it being better or worse than you'd like to think it is.

Focus on what your real strengths and weaknesses are. Most importantly develop a relationship with your own still silent presence within.

Pay more attention to the part of you which is always connected to the source of the universe. Pay more attention to the part of you that is unmoving, creative intelligence. This will resolve a lot of previously perceived issues and will simplify your journey into badassery.

What you focus on grows. Choose consciously for that which serves you in your awakening.

Protect your relationship with that still, silent presence. Protect whatever is truly serving you in the reestablishment of life lived in the present moment.

Principle Seven

It's not all "light and love". Shadow work is uncomfortable and messy, but super crucial. What you don't see will unconsciously run your life.

What is the Shadow? The shadow is where we have repressed or suppressed parts of ourselves which we were taught aren't acceptable in order to be successful, loved, included.

What do we find here? Often it is our brilliance, our neediness, our charisma, our passion, our innocence, our vulnerability, our boundaries, our hurt, anger, fear.

Some of us learn that being honest is dangerous. Some of us learn the exact opposite.

In our youth we experienced a variety of hurts and messages that made us believe there was something wrong with us. Some of it was extreme trauma; some of it was incessantly being teased. Some of it was more subtle.

We felt too smart, too silly, too beautiful, too wild, too passionate, too powerful, too loud, too full-on.

There are variations to what is held therein, but primarily it is the same for us all. We all experienced parts of us being pushed aside into the creation of this shadow.

This suppression makes us take inefficient pathways to try to get our needs met. Of course it doesn't work out very well, leaving us feeling flat, resigned, stifled, and unfulfilled.

Every human resists leaning into the shadow and yet craves being free enough to let it be seen. You will never be free enough to be fully present to your life if you continue to avoid this. Be willing to look at what's behind your curtain.

This is the ultimate self-love move. You won't find monsters but a scared child needing assurance that it is safe to come out and be whole now.

Allowing the Shadow to be seen heals the habits of shyness and reluctance to be fully present to your life. As you continue on including your whole self, notice that your capacity to be present increases exponentially.

Principle Eight

You must become a finder of experience and be willing to let go of the spiritual seeker voice in your head measuring your growth. This is the most essential principle! OMG.

There's a voice in our head that sounds just like us that we're dependent on all day long.

If you have sat still with yourself for any period of time, you may begin to notice that you talk to yourself in your head and that it is incessant, continuous.

There are lots of thoughts that we have, but ultimately underneath it all there's a commentator that's assessing everything.

Have you noticed this yet?
If you have not yet noticed this, you must sit still long enough to recognize it, and one meditation session of 10 to 20 minutes, with the intention to notice, should do the trick.

You can also become aware of it with your eyes open if you're surrendered enough. This is why I add in different Exercises here for you to explore - so when I say keep your eyes open, it is in part, for this end result.

You need to see that it's happening all the time. And when you do see it, you'll feel overwhelmed as though there's no way possible to reverse such an insidious habit. But there is.

Instead of looking at it like a chore or like an impossibility, it's best to look at it like a really fun game.

It's so important that you recognize this commentator is not just talking to you about your to-do list; it's also talking to you about how you aren't good enough; it's also talking to you about how great you're doing; it is the same mechanism, the same voice, even though it may appear that they are different.

For the purposes of expansion of consciousness, any voice in the head is a mechanism of the movement of the mind and has nothing to do with your own pure presence. It is separate from that, and it must be seen as such.

Until you see the commentator you will be listening to it when it tells you you're not doing great, and you will listen to it when it tells you that you are doing great. You will be on the rollercoaster.

You see, even when you pay attention to it telling you that you are doing great, you're **feeding your habit of paying attention to it**. And therefore it does not serve.

The ego cannot assist itself and rise out of ignorance. The mind cannot transcend itself. Only by changing your relationship to what you are identifying with can you transcend this habit.

One of the most dangerous voices I've come across- and this was very surprising and irritating to me initially - is the voice of the spiritual teacher, spiritual cheerleader, the voice of the spiritual monitor in there trying to make sure I was doing the right thing on the right track, constantly using effort and energy to assess my growth.

Thank God for the day that I finally heard my teacher say that this was still the voice of the ego, still a movement of the mind and that I shouldn't pay attention to it.

Since I have been practicing no longer paying any attention to it, I have experienced vast amounts of freedom that were not there previously.

I have experienced far greater ease and effortlessness in my experience of being present as a result of changing my relationship to the commentator. I recommend that you give it a go.

Understanding the Purpose

A human being has the potential to evolve into higher states of consciousness. Applying what you are learning and doing will unfold this destiny. It's Science.

Experiencing higher consciousness for yourself is what matters. No one can give it to you through words - or in any other way. Being open to this as reality is important only if you are interested in making your life about the badass adventure of embodying these states.

Doing your own investigative research will enlighten you to what Science, both ancient and modern, reveals to you.

You don't have to believe it. Belief happens in the 10% thinking level of the mind - not in the experience of resting present to what is. So....who cares what you believe? Belief is by nature limiting.

Being open to recognizing your own experience is the opposite.
Let's adjust belief here.

You have got to be open to experiencing, and you have got to be willing to do what it takes to gain experience.

You are not qualified to train yourself - doing so will lead you in circles as it has done all your life. Why? Because you will be relying on the voice in your mind to lead you out of that level of consciousness, and that is never ever going to work.

You must be curious and humble enough to try to apply what has proven effective for those who've gone before you.

Follow in the sure footsteps of those who've done the work, exercised the muscle, gone through the training, been held accountable by a qualified teacher.

If you are freaked out, that is totally cool. Every important step I ever take scares the shit out of me - at least a little bit. At the very least it is exhilarating.

If you are freaked out but willing - man, kudos to you! You are my kind of people! THAT is what it takes. Feel the freak and do it anyway!

Now begins the meticulous but wonderful task of replacing that habit with a new one.

What is this new habit? Turning attention within.

KeyPoints

★ Certain mindset shifts are helpful to begin the playful engagement with meditation, consciousness and the present moment.

★ You have been conditioned into a state of victim consciousness - typical in the waking state. Life is not happening to you, it is happening for you. You can and will move into a different state where this becomes apparent.

★ No thought, feeling, circumstance, belonging, not even the body belong to you. They belong to the Divine. You are a privileged steward and observer.

★ The Universe exists to serve you in your awakening and therefore is set up to appear to fail you when you are heading in the wrong direction, or when something no longer serves.

★ Suffering is optional. Pain, discomfort, challenge, and circumstances beyond control are inevitable. AS one evolves, it is apparent that suffering is not the same as these.

★ Your birthright was and is presence. What you focus on expands.

★ The Shadow is where wholeness lies. Welcome it all here, as is.

★ Recover from seeking. Discover and root in experiential finding of the present moment.

★ Belief is not required here. Belief happens in the 10% thinking level of the mind. Do the things herein and observe the results. The proof is in the pudding.

Quest Goals

★   Go back through each of the above Principles. Be present to each of the points in this chapter and feel into.

Notice how foreign they may be, how much they resonate or how you see you have room to grow into them. Observe any resistance to them. Observe any part that lights you up.

No need to analyze - just notice and then write down anything you wish to at this time.

Your Aura is So Dope

You radiate such light. You are so beautiful. Did you know that? I can hardly take my attention from you, you divine thing. How'd you get an Aura like that? You have something about you... There is a light in your eyes. You have some depth to you that is startling - I am almost frightened. But I want more. How do I get closer to you? And do you see me? Do you recognize me too? Do you feel anything even remotely similar? I don't even know what I'm seeing so probably not - but my, are you an alluring creature. Please tell me what I need to do to be in your Aura. How do you get it so peaceful and yummy? Your energy is so solid, powerful, here. You are so real, so raw. Your laughter though! It's almost disturbing how authentic you are. What do I do to get an Aura like that?
It's so Dope!

Meditation

"The Soul loves to meditate, for in contact with the spirit lies its greatest joy." - Paramahansa Yogananda

"A man lives in slavery without meditation because he lives unconsciously. He lives like a robot. Meditation starts changing you. It transforms your unconsciousness into consciousness... It is the only alchemy which transforms the raw energy into a refined world of mysteries." - Osho

Meditation Defined

We are going to look at different definitions of meditation out there because I have one way of looking at it - from a scientific lens, and I want you to understand what I mean when I say "meditation" as well as what I do not mean.

Wikipedia's Definition:

Meditation is a practice where an individual uses a technique such as mindfulness, or focusing the mind on a particular object, thought, or activity to train attention and awareness, and achieve a mentally clear and emotionally calm and stable state. Scholars have found meditation difficult to define, as practices vary both between traditions and within them.

Medical Dictionary Defines Meditation:

Definition: Meditation is a practice of concentrated focus upon a sound, object, visualization, the breath, movement, or attention itself in order to increase awareness of the present moment, reduce stress, promote relaxation, and enhance personal and spiritual growth.

Purpose: Meditation benefits people with or without acute medical illness or stress. People who meditate regularly have been shown to feel less anxiety and depression. They also report that they experience more enjoyment and appreciation of life and that their relationships with others are improved. Meditation produces a state of deep relaxation and a sense of balance or equanimity.

Definition by The Yoga Sutras: (An Ancient Spiritual Science text of the Himalayan Region) *Enlightenment A New Translation and Commentary (on) the Yoga Sutras of Patanjali* by Maharishi Sadashiva Isham

Pada I. Sutra I.
Atha yoga anushasanam
Now, the teaching of Yoga (Yoga translated means to yoke, unite - union)

"The Science of Yoga (union) begins and ends in the present moment." "...the present instant is at once the goal and the means of the Science of Union." Meditation is "the repeated sequence of experiencing the Now over and over again until it becomes permanent." "When the mind stills its noisy activity, consciousness experiences the Now, which is eternal peace...By repeating this experience over and over, the mind becomes habituated to the Silence and stays there permanently, even in the midst of the most dynamic activity."

Pada I. Sutra 2.
Yogas' chitta vritti nirodhah
Yoga (Union) is consciousness with its movements still.

"The natural condition of the mind is silence." "If we wish the mind to still, introduction of strain or effort will not serve us." "What is required to still the mind is an object of attention that charms the mind, thereby allowing it to settle down to more and more universal and silent levels of functioning. This object could take any number of possible (meditative) forms, but the one universal requirement...must be that it is increasingly effortless." "There are only three requirements (to meditate effectively, re-establishing life in the present moment). There must be 1) a functioning nervous system, capable of thought. There must also be 2) a suitable vehicle for the mind to follow in this process of stilling, a vehicle which naturally and effortlessly pulls the mind inward to ever deeper levels of silence, until even the faintest level of activity is Ascended...And there also needs to be 3) competent guidance to ensure the necessary feedback that verifies the correctness of the practice."

My Experience

"Meditation is the state of no-mind - not of a silent mind, not of a healthy mind, not of a concentrated mind, no. Meditation is the state of no-mind: no society within you, no conditioning within you - just you, with you - pure consciousness." - Osho

I remember reading a meditation book when I was like 18. I tried to do what it said.

The little East Indian man with long hair, beard and robe sat in lotus position on the page. The instruction said: "watch thoughts like clouds floating by."

I sat for probably a total of 5 minutes (if that) and thought, "what in the hell are they talking about - there's no clouds in here - only me!"

I was on to something - I would find out much later and here's what it was:

1: There is a whole lot of "ME ME ME" in the movement of the mind and

2: Everyone who begins meditation can't yet see that their thoughts, feelings, sensation, circumstances are not them. This phenomenon is normal. It also changes over time.

This experience pushed me to find a real practice that would not only anchor me inward, but also would offer me a lot of support. I just knew that left to my own, there was no way I was going to recognize the subtleties of the voices in my head.

I could barely discern them even after two years of practice. I had to practice sitting silently with discomfort, thoughts, feelings, body sensations, and the outside exactly as it is.

Sometimes silence comes upon the mind. Much of the time in meditation, it appears that there are thoughts and the other movement intermittent with whichever technique you are using.

I needed a 6-month meditation retreat and teacher training process to really get some space in the mind and clarity about how to be present.

Not everyone needs this to get traction, confidence and stability in the experience. It seems to me that unless people are practicing consistently with an effective tool and have the peer and mentor support to keep going, it is a small percentage who get the confidence to choose to continue.

Today's World

Thankfully meditation has become a part of the mainstream culture - it is en vogue. It has become a popular tool and prescription given by doctors and therapists for people healing from anxiety, depression, addiction, trauma and less intense challenges to establish and maintain wellbeing.

We now have so much good modern Science showing proof of things yogis and ninjas have always known. For example we now have modern proof that a consistent meditation practice decreases stress hormones and increases healthy happy hormones and beyond.

Meditation has become popular in the Health & Fitness industry for improving physical health, performance, a general increase in vitality, and the Science pointing to an increase in longevity.

Meditation has become popular in the business and personal development world as it has been proven effective to increase job satisfaction, focus, productivity, creativity, cooperation, efficiency and willingness to be teachable.

Meditation has been a fundamental element in most every spiritual or religious group on the planet, bringing people into a richer relationship with a higher power.

This is the primary reason I began my meditation practice. Little did I know that I'd get all of these other benefits too. Many things I was seeking to avoid meditation would force me to face, welcome, and change my relationship with.

Meditation would elicit all manner of healing response. Not always comfortable, clean ones. I learned there was enough patience, spaciousness and courage in me for that.

Where once I meant to kill the ego, meditation forced me to sit and make friends with it. Meditation and direction from my teacher revealed clearly what the ego actually is and put it in its proper, useful place.

Meditation made me befriend and honor myself, thereby increasing my ability to love and be loved.

The focus changed. It isn't about becoming a better person, but about playfully exploring being present and helping others to do the same.

The badassery comes from continuing on with innocence, curiosity, willingness to be teachable, present to what is now - not living inside of the insight I received in any other moment.

The results are so badass: purpose, connection, joy and aliveness for no reason at all. It's so humbling.

Purposes of Meditation

Life begins inside of a beautiful state of freedom.

Life experience leaves us with certain impressions of who we are, who we are not, how to get through this life with efficiency, effectiveness and resilience.

We begin to believe we are limited to this conditioned way. We unconsciously begin believing that the mind's beliefs, as well as the body and its sensations, are what we are. We pay more attention to the mind and less to intuitive presence.

But we are not the movement of the mind. We are the presence witness to it. When we are taught to identify our thoughts and analyze the outer and inner experience of life, we are habituating a constant state of thinking.

This is an active state where we cannot rest - the body never rests in this analysis mode. We are taught, encouraged and rewarded for thinking well.

We forget that we are that which is watching, aware of thoughts, with zero opinion or comment - simple awareness. We identify with the mind and forget we ever lived in the innocent witnessing and experiencing of life.

We know from Quantum Physics and other Sciences that what we put our focus on grows; it is enhanced in our life. We take on the beliefs or the rejection of the beliefs held by our family & society and this shapes who we believe ourselves to be.

Helpful for a time in our development, but then, in fact crippling us from all we could be. There comes a point in everyone's life where we know that there is more - and we seek it.

Sometimes we seek this something more unconsciously through food, sex, drugs, alcohol, keeping busy, working a ton, excess in anything or numbing out in any way - to find relief, peace, connection, okayness.

We produce more stress hormones as we habitually try to be one thing or to avoid being something else. This is not comfortable.

Some of us find great addictions to try to counter the insanity and discomfort of this habit. We call it unplugging from and unwinding when in reality almost every popular way out there of doing so is not unplugging at all.

Instead, these things deepen the state of ignorance, adding stress to the nervous system, habituating unconsciousness and leaving zero room for the possibility, capacity or reality of aliveness, joy, and peace of mind.

We intuitively know what we are after, but don't have the right tools, or understanding. So we seek relief and connection in numbing out.

It's like this - we know we should brush our teeth and floss a few times a day for maintenance of our gum and tooth health. We know we don't want plaque and tartar to build up, creating tooth decay, gum diseases or tooth loss. Right?

What meditators understand and Science shows is that the majority of the population does not understand that meditation, like dental care, gives us certain desirable and highly probable, consistent results and helps us to avoid certain undesirable results.

The use of a really viable meditative tool helps us to avoid energetic, physical and emotional overloading of stress and all of its various resulting dis-ease. Meditation helps us to reverse the incessant and unconscious habit of thinking. Meditation can help us to stop numbing out through other addictions too.

Meditation is the way to plug into the truest form of relief and protection that there is: pure conscious presence. Practicing meditation and being present results in a sense of fulfillment, purpose, connection and wholeness. Meditation is the pathway to discovering our true nature - badassery.

Hooray for the moment we go "Universe! Take me now or show me another way." And the way always presents itself. Whether we have the capacity in that moment to claim it or not is another thing.

Meditation is a powerful key to strengthen your capacity. Meditation removes whatever parts of you and habits of the mind that are in the way of your capacity to seek and find something more.

Meditation begins to develop a state of being where all of that conditioning rights itself. Every area of life improves because you are living anchored in the present moment and in your fullest potential.

We don't find lasting happiness from working on every area of life - never. That approach has always led me to a sense of insufficiency, lack, the need for more, better, rather than peace, purpose and holiness.

Happiness is a natural by-product of changing the relationship with the critic and commentator in the mind and by developing an awareness of this moment.

Meditation returns us to our original state of innocence as we commune with the present moment. We do not have to try to make that happen. We practice shifting attention - taking ourselves out of the vibe and channel of our normal mode of operation.

This simple practice puts inside of the greatest alchemizing force - the source of all you seek, all you are, and all that can and will transform your life. Don't take my word for that. Explore this for yourself.

Contemplative Exercise

Pause to reflect and maybe even journal on the below musings.

Does it seem doable to develop the muscle, aware of inner silence, beginning to recognize it and effortlessly maintain awareness of it?

What would it be like to stabilize that level of consciousness?

Do you believe it is a possibility for an average person like you to do so?

Is it possible for one who has devoted time to meditation and spirituality but is living in the real world with responsibilities and busyness?

Do you believe that this is a real thing and attainable by anyone? Or do you see a belief in you that this type of state or reality is reserved for the likes of Buddha and Jesus , the Dalai Lama - you know - the *real deal* folks?

As you've paused to reflect on the above and journaled on this - if you'd be so bold, go share with us what you've discovered in the **Rock Your Mind Global** Facebook group. And by the way... Dude- you are the real deal folks. Or you could be.

I don't know if you've made the switch from being a seeker to finder yet - from being a poser to being an effortless transmitter of presence - of humble badassery.

In one way this adventure is not for the faint-of-heart dabblers who are content to keep posing in life.

For sure making this inner switch from being a seeker to becoming a finder is the only possibility if you are interested in really getting anywhere in terms of consciously living life in the present moment.

What Meditation Isn't

- Meditation is not a belief system.
- Meditation is not a mood.
- Meditation isn't a religious practice - though it can be an essential spiritual practice.
- Meditation is not airy fairy voodoo. Meditation isn't about auras, angels, or psychic ability.
- Meditation is not just a relaxation technique.

Many other practices are lumped together with meditation such as:
- Visualization
- Prayer
- Shamanic Journeying
- Guided Meditation

These practices are beautiful and can help heal a brain and a body. These practices can help relax a person and help a person feel a greater sense of connection. They can be very enjoyable and interesting to the mind. These practices may even explore subtle levels of the mind.

They are not at all proficient, however, at helping one transcend the mind.

Most of these practices are dependent upon the facilitator and so not at all empowering to practitioners.

In my experience, these types of practices leave little room for clear awareness of how one is habitually and consistently leaving the present moment. Nor do they leave any room for the practitioner to recognize the living experience of being present.

These practices can truly help certain demographics of people to feel better and have a better life. I share some of these types of practices with my students and in the work I do as a healer.

They serve wonderful purposes, but they do not offer the simple yet profound transcendence that the essence of this book and every teaching of the One offers.

For the purposes of evolution into higher states of consciousness and for the purposes of this book, when we talk about Meditation, I do not ever mean any of these types of practices.

NOTE: I know this will seem ironic or even hypocritical. For example, I lead guided experiences in meditation.

However, I am not here to encourage dependence on me.

I am here to hold your hand into a state where you can sit silently transcending fear and limitation, becoming clear about your own presence, connection to Source and ability to be present.

I am here to offer resources, my own experience and continuing education suggestions for those who are hungry for these. I am here to empower you into your own self-mastery and transcendence.

A silent seated practice allows the practitioner to discover inner, silent presence as clearly and efficiently as possible. This type of practice is most desirable in achieving stable awareness of the present moment and in transcending the typical stressed-out human state.

Sacred Pause

Deep Breath Time.
Rest Back. Be 100% Here.

If you are a person who has been into practices just mentioned, you may be getting touchy right now.

I would get that. But let me ask you something... Why are you still seeking a meditation practice or meditation support, if what you are doing is consistently producing what you deeply crave?

There are different types of meditative practices on the planet.

I know of very few which consistently give people the result of discovering inner silence, seeing one's own true nature, mastering one's habits of the mind. And effectively re-establishing life lived in the present moment.

Have whatever practices you want to have. Understand which is for what purpose though.

Commit to this exploration, for a time, if you are at all interested in your awakened human destiny, just to see for yourself what the experience is like.

Physical + Mental Benefits of Meditation

Some benefits of a meditation practice of getting yourself to sit down and close your eyes begin with a level of self-respect in that you are disciplining yourself first to sit and second to bring your attention back to the point of focus for meditation over and over again.

I am one of the least disciplined people naturally as a free-spirit and visionary and muse.

However, the discipline that comes from practice in these two ways alone has given me a grounding sense of freedom and clarity and effectiveness, creativity and intelligence, connection, purpose and self-love that I didn't expect at all - and maybe was unconsciously way too afraid to even begin to hope little old flaky me could cultivate. But I have. And I still am a free-spirit.

Besides the self-respect that comes along with discipline, I have healed many and found manageability in the rest of the ptsd symptoms and presentations in my mind, body and life.

That's not to say that the quirk they presented in me is gone. I am quirky to be sure. But I am no longer being strangled by the anxiety, fear, depression, extreme effort to try to fit in, to not let anyone see my struggle, the addiction to analyzing, being swept up in emotion, alcohol, people's approval and attention, and as many forms of self-sabotage.

Mine may be an extreme example.

Maybe you don't know what that kind of life is like. Maybe you just have a little normal stress you are trying to manage. Maybe you are here because your psychiatrist said it would help. Maybe the doc said it could help lower your blood pressure.

Maybe your yoga teacher suggested it would enhance your ability to be present in class, limiting the chance of hurting yourself and increasing awareness and enjoyment.

Maybe you had an experience once, one you coin "spiritual" and you are curious if you can get something like that back.

All of these benefits and outcomes have been my direct experience of practice.

Simply feeling comfortable in my own skin was a HUGE blessing. Getting to a place where I could truly be useful to anyone else is a MIRACLE.

But BOTH are absolutely the experience of any devoted practitioner. It is important for you to know why you are here reading this book and seeking to employ its suggestions.

Why do you want to meditate?
What will it give you? Remember your why and recommit over and over. Share it - in conversation, in your prayers, to your mentor,

to your partner, your kids, your co-workers. Get clear. Be clear. Remain clear.

Potential Benefits of Meditation

★ Reduces Pain ★ Lowers blood pressure ★ Heals respiratory illnesses including sinus, allergy and asthma issues (I have a direct experience of this and could go more into the science of potential and likely why's but not here) ★ Strengthens Immune System ★ Improves Digestion (the source of all health) ★ Assists the body in healing more quickly from lifelong, acute, or new issues ★ Anti-inflammatory effect ★ Reduces or significantly improves menstrual or menopausal issues ★ Regulates mood disorders ★ Reduces anger ★ Reduces anxiety, depression and stress ★ Reduces and even heals PTSD symptoms ★ Improves self-esteem, increase self-love ★ Supports the healing of addictions ★ Increase creativity, focus, efficiency ★ Increase many forms of self-awareness ★ Improves working memory (though...my mind not so much!) ★ Improves sleep ★ Increases ability to work in stressful situations ★ Improves ability to make better decisions,and solve problems ★ Helps you learn - to be open to and less resistant to learning new things and put your mind in a place to be ready to learn new things ★ Decreases feelings of loneliness, increases a sense of connection ★ Opens us to vulnerability, authenticity, and compassion ★ Increases sense of spiritual connection to inner self, life, others and a higher power

Special Note RE: Mental Health

Even though meditation can be useful in assisting people heal mental health issues, PTSD and addiction, there are stages and certain diagnoses where meditation and meditative therapies and practices can increase or exacerbate the problem, and even at times, destroy long-term progress that was made.

I have unfortunately come across this in students and clients of mine and had to learn the hard way that mental health, ptsd, addiction treatment and even brain injury should be treated by physicians and licensed therapists alone and that no one in these categories should explore and meditation practice (or anything like it) on their own but under the direct instruction and supervision of the healthcare provider. Period.

I fell into these categories and found healing, so you may likely as well. However, the things I have seen in people who just should not have had meditation as a part of their regimen was intense, scary, toxic, overwhelming and sad.

Some folks are in very fragile spaces and meditation can definitely increase psychosis, insanity, dissociation, etc... please consult your healthcare and mental-health care provider.

I am not a doctor and I am not offering medical nor mental health advice here. Simply sharing my own experience and knowledge of 20 years. Please consult your wellness team if you've been diagnosed or suspect you may have mental health and trauma issues.

Common Erroneous Beliefs in the Way of Meditation

I have met a vast number of humans who believe they cannot meditate - whether they have tried it or not. And I LOVE de-bunking, de-mystifying and otherwise (and most importantly) guiding folks into their own experience of meditation. It's a privilege to witness the emergence of confidence, clarity and conviction around meditating, being present, and in general, a badass experience of life.

So, what are the things that these folks often say about how they know they cannot meditate?

You know what they are because you've come up against them yourself at some point.

See if you can relate to any of these...

"My mind is too busy"
"I don't know what to do"
"I just can't sit like that"

The first point below is by far the number one issue people believe that they have. There is an entire section dedicated to this topic called "Thoughts" so I do not address it further in this section.

Not Knowing What to Do

Have you ever tried something new? Are you the sort that fakes it until you make it? Or do you avoid new things?

Do you look at all of the instructions before you begin the new thing, sometimes procrastinating indefinitely?

Do you jump in reading instructions and using intuition as you go?

It seems like the best approach in a meditation practice and in learning how to live life in the present moment is to jump in, applying instruction immediately.

It seems to work well to trust that you can't do it wrong. It works well to be teachable, to be curious, and to keep going. It works well to share what you are experiencing and any doubts you have with someone who has gone before you. The right instruction and support can go a long way.

Bottom line though is: You cannot do it wrong. You don't have to know much- just apply, engage, do it now!

Right Posture

I do hope that most of you do not think that you have to sit in the "lotus position" to practice meditation.

Yet, I cannot tell you how many people have told me that they can't do meditation because of this.

Do you know that if you are cutting off your circulation during meditation, your brain will increase activity to get you to move and allow the flow of blood?

HA! I'm totally cracking up over here. Don't sit like that.

And if you do and you need to move, for goodness sake move and continue on meditating. Lord have mercy.

There is something to be said about what happens when I practice lying down and my body thinks it is time to sleep, or when I practice sitting upright where there is more alertness. There is a halfway point there too where grogginess will happen.

Don't be lazy. Geez.

Upright and alert is best to actually say you were meditating. This uprightness can be achieved in an armchair, office chair, dining chair, sitting against the wall, a tree, another person - even propped up with pillows in your bed.

Physiology plays an important role in practice. Which is why sitting in the lotus position or on the floor on a meditation cushion may be the exact wrong choice for many body-types.

Even though I can meditate in lotus or on a cushion for an hour or more with very little movement, I don't have to in order to attain growth of consciousness, so I don't.

These types of rigid postures can train one into being very focused. It is true, but it's a very outdated method of motivation by extremes or pain.

I'm so over that. Aren't you?

Some of the longest standing traditions around come with some extraneous practices including physical posture, beliefs, and ritual. Those external trappings may be what you need to be committed to a practice. That's fine. But they are not actually universally needed and can in fact get in the way of transcending the waking state consciousness.

Keep it real, people. I know hundreds of people who don't ever take those external things on, but instead are absolute in their devotion to exploring the conscious space that thoughts and all of life manifest through.

These types appear to evolve far more efficiently and joyfully than anyone I know doing it in a more strict and dogmatic sort of way. They have made this mythic adventure about one thing, rather than about doing many things right to get there.

But hey if you want to sit like that and it fuels you to go for it, then please keep it up!

For the rest of you who have come up against this as a roadblock because of knees, hips, weight, back and other issues, breathe that sigh of relief and never pay attention to this misconception again. So yay - no deal - right?

Identified with You

All the comings and goings of this life Trying to figure out if I was smart enough or pretty enough or cool enough.

Discerning erroneously - by the circumstances in my life whether I had any value in this world

Seeking a reason, a purpose - for why I exist.

All the education telling me how to think, what was important to know, which career path to take.

What sort of thinker or feeler I am.

Prompting me toward which box can I identify with the most.

Who in the hell decided all of this garbage mattered? Why didn't they teach me how to pay attention to You? Why didn't they teach me that my only identity should be as Your vessel? Why didn't they prioritize this lesson, course, degree?

I realize from here, that they could not. It was not part of the current design. Not part of Your clever plan.

Yet, all of this noise and conditioning - pure distraction to the palpable fullness of Your grace. I get to be so many things in this surrendered state.

My inner focus fixed upon You, I am free to be whatever You would have me be.

Free to do whatever You would have me do.

Free to know - in true gnosis - to the core of consciousness and to the bones of this physical frame: The only identity ever needed, the only one that is sane or even real, is the identification with You.

Thoughts

"The most decisive event in your life is when you discover you are not your thoughts or emotions. Instead, you can be present as the awareness behind the thoughts and emotions." - Eckhart Tolle

Yes.
Thoughts have their own chapter.
Why?
Because they are the number one reason people think that they can not meditate. I'd like for you to hear me now - and then do the research for yourself.

Thoughts can not stop or even slow the process of meditation - unless you make a deal out of them, people. Thoughts are a part of life and a part of meditation.

When you change your relationship with your mind - with thought, you will laugh at how you have been trying to manage movement of thought and how impossible that is - like trying to lasso the wind.

You will see, as you make your practice more interesting to you than whether or not you are having thought, that thoughts are the wrong focus.

The part of you that is aware of thought is where your holy grail lies. Everything you've been missing is therein. This recognition takes practice. Thankfully we've got our whole lives to play with this.

To start with, I'd like to unpack thoughts, thinking and awareness of other types of experiences in an effort to support you in feeling safe enough to quit wasting time around thought and start focusing on what actually matters.

To transcend, we first must see.
So here we go...

A Busy Mind

We hear that meditation helps to clear the mind.

What we believe this statement is saying is: "you are supposed to clear your mind when you meditate."

See the distinction?

Read the above over again until it is clear.
It's a CRUCIAL distinction.

The idea that **you** are supposed to still your mind and be without thoughts is just a mass erroneous belief.

The mind is busy until it isn't.

Does meditation help or produce a clearing of or a quieting of the mind - yes.

Is that always how it is when a person like myself is sitting there (after 21 years of practice) NO.

Do I care?
Nope.

I wouldn't bother to waste one second even thinking about caring.

Do I believe it determines how good my meditation is? No.

Ultimately, how many thoughts I have during meditation - few or a barrage - is not interesting to me at all.

Did I also believe that I didn't know what to do, upon hearing that I was supposed to clear the mind during meditation? Of course.

I do not know anyone who has attempted it from this particular direction who has succeeded.

I was taught that movement in the mind should be looked at as stress healing in the nervous system.

I've observed this phenomenon long enough to say this assessment seems to be true.

And like dust in a dustpan, my focus is on the clean floor, not what I just swept up. If the above notion is in any way true, thought should not be a focus.

Thoughts come and go and are welcome to do so. They should not be interesting to you.

Be interested in the tool and the practice. Be curious about what the meditative tool is revealing.

The space through which the thoughts are showing up becomes more apparent, attractive and real. That space is where magic, beauty, connection, freedom, oneness reside.

Thoughts are way less interesting and enjoyable than this conscious space. The space will become a divine magnet. Like an enamoured lover, it will bewitch and bless you in spades beyond what any thought ever could.

Let's Break it Down

Thoughts are a part of life and a part of meditation.

Not like, you know, thoughts are a part of meditation only until you become a master.

Thoughts are a part of meditation, period.

Can you ever stop thoughts during meditation? Have YOU?

I tried to. Zoiks. Forget about it.

However, over the years of paying more attention to inner stillness, there are times when I have no idea if a thought or emotion could ever arise because I am immersed in awareness of stillness.

It is riveting and I could care less - impossible to even care or notice. I can choose to pay more attention to stillness, so I do.

And - at this time, I continue to have thoughts. Sometimes a lot. Sometimes few. And I do not care.

What are thoughts and how are they formed?

You could say that thoughts are digested material. Or dust in the dustpan.

You could say that they are smoke coming from the fire of what you've perceived in any past moment all being released, let go of, being moved on from.

Thoughts are proof that release has happened.

I know, I know. Radical, right?

You've been taught that thoughts are something important that you should be paying attention to. It's how you've measured your success and your identity.

The problem is most of the thoughts coming through are not genius intuition. They are regurgitations, reiterations; they are stale, old, not life-affirming, not life-producing, nor brilliant.

In general humans have 60,000-90,000 thoughts in a day and most are the same thoughts we've had for years. The same storylines and underlying beliefs.

Identified with these streams of thought and not even knowing it, we create the same limitations and challenges, the same quality of life, the same levels of resolve. And we never see it.

We are unaware because we are too busy paying attention to the content of the thought streams. We never break this pattern until we change our relationship with the mind, until we transcend into a new level of consciousness.

What is it That Thoughts are Trying to Achieve?

Thoughts aren't trying to do anything. They do not have intelligence. They are a result of life being perceived by the senses, by life being digested by the brain.

Electric impulses, energy otherwise known as Qi, or life force energy moving, a puff of smoke.

Isn't that crazy?

That is what thoughts are. They are not trying to achieve anything because they are not intelligent.

You have an intelligence, but it is not thoughts. Intelligence is the part of you which is aware of thoughts.

How are Thoughts Related to Meditation?

Obviously if you close your eyes and sit there doing nothing you will notice those 60,000+ thoughts. They will come and go.
You will practice focusing on your meditative tool and begin to recognize that part of you that is noticing thought.

Thoughts, Emotions + Body Sensations

Have you ever noticed that you can dramatize and increase a situation with the words you say and the story you weave in your mind?

Have you ever noticed that you can stop the crazies by shifting your focus away from the sensation of emotion, off from the story in your head, off from attraction to fuel the whole thing?

I have done a lot of research. I've paid close attention. Being out of the moment, unconscious, paying attention to thoughts leaves us weak.

We are susceptible to not even notice that we are making issues bigger than they are - oftentimes adding fuel to a fire of suffering.

Paying attention to and continuing on with thought streams also can and does absolutely increase physical sensations of pain, the physical symptoms of anxiety and asthma attacks, the crushing sense of overwhelm, and pleasant sensations as well.

Emotions will come and go; pain in the body may stick around - but paying attention to the thoughts around emotions and sensations, the story in the mind about the emotion or sensation, will accentuate, expand, give energy to, make it more real and more out of control.

That's powerful, isn't it?

If we can unconsciously exacerbate emotions and sensations, we can consciously allow them to come and go without cultivating suffering. We can consciously choose to put more of our attention on spaciousness, gravity, the breath, the quality of peace, anything we can praise or be grateful for.

We can change the unconscious habit of suffering caused by paying too much attention to the emotion or sensation by putting more attention to the space they are showing up within. We can stop ourselves from paying attention to, or feeding any story around, the energy moving through us.

We can stop identifying with thoughts, feelings, and emotions. We can become aware of what we are doing unconsciously, and when we see it happening we can do something different.

The Current Relationship to Thought + What it Could Be

In our current relationship with thought, there is no separation. We are what we think. There is no space.

With the practice of meditation space is created. In that space, our true self is revealed. This part of us is presence, is consciousness, is intuitive intelligence. The silent and still part of us has no thought, no emotion, and no troubles.

We begin to notice, get familiar with, and develop a robust relationship with that still silent presence. This new habit replaces the old relationship with thought.

Thought, emotion and circumstance can do whatever they want to do. We keep still.

We can change our relationship with the movement of the mind, with the movement of emotions, with the movement of life as we practice meditation and being present.

We can create a healthier, more sane relationship with all that movement. One where we are not glued to the rollercoaster and not so impacted by it. One where we are the absolute witness to the movement, identified with the inner still, silent presence.

The mind goes to work for us to be utilized as it is needed. It is put in its right place. We stop being dragged around in a drone-like state by it. Doable and wonderful.

What is the difference between thoughts and thinking? + How to notice the difference between having a thought and thinking

As you begin to observe more keenly, you will realize that thoughts bubble up but then quickly dissolve.

Or they arise and you pay your attention to them. You may notice that when you pay attention to them you quickly identify with them. Once this happens you begin talking to yourself formulating endless streams of thought.

There is a difference between a thought and thinking. Thoughts arise. Our attention and engagement creates streams of thought.

For the purposes of meditating, choosing to not consciously engage thinking is part of the instruction.

Thoughts will come and go. Do your best to let them do so by focusing on meditative technique instead.

For the purposes of being present, and this is a different level of badassery, be present rather than engaging thinking.

You'll have thoughts. Expect that.

You'll cultivate the ability to observe them and consciously choose to be carried forward without having to engage thinking.

That may seem confusing to your mind, but your mind is not the thing that is going to really get this, so it doesn't matter. Don't worry, this will come clear as you gain experience in practice.

So what is the take away here?

Thoughts are always okay.
Just don't think. And when you do find that you are thinking, treat this realization as the universe's meditation bell bringing you back to your meditation technique, to the present moment. Cool, right?

KeyPoints

★   Thoughts are a natural part of meditation.

★   Having a lot of thoughts during meditation is common - but also erroneously believed to be a problem. It is the #1 reason people give up on themselves and their practice. Having thoughts is proof that you are alive. Proof that you are healing stress. Having a lot of thoughts does NOT mean that you aren't meditating correctly.

★   Thoughts are different from thinking. Try not to entertain thoughts as they will turn into thinking which turns into illusion and being a drone.

★ Treat all thoughts as non-important and pay more attention to your meditation technique or to inner silence, or to the space that the thoughts are moving through

★ You are not your thoughts - though you've been trained to believe that you are. You are that which is peacefully aware of the thoughts.

★ To change your relationship with your thoughts, simply shift attention to your practice.

Quest Goals

★ Pay attention to how many times you judge the fact that you are experiencing thoughts - especially the ones that you wish would go away and never come back. You want to see this so you can know for yourself what you are doing. With this awareness you can then make a choice to refocus attention.

★ If you are already practicing meditation, notice how often you wince or judge when thoughts seem to be bombarding you - and remember that you can relax about this. Put more attention immediately on your practice.

★   Consider your current or lifelong relationship with thoughts and thinking. Does it seem impossible to you to establish a state where you aren't thinking nearly as much? Does it seem unrealistic or even dangerous to you to not think so much?

★   Consider what your heart's desire is around peace of mind. Does it include not thinking so damn much? What would happen if you weren't so attached to thinking about everything but instead were able to be present to it? What fears do you see around this? Are they founded? What blessings can you see around this? What space and peace might you have in your experience?

★   Are you ready to accept that thoughts are not a problem in meditation?

★   Are you ready to accept that you don't have to do anything with your thoughts but allow them to be a sign of healing taking place, of stress burning up?

★   Are you ready to make your focal point in practice more interesting and important than thoughts in regard to meditation?

PART THREE

CULTIVATE CONGRUENT CONDITIONS OF BADASSERY

Meditate

"In the midst of movement and chaos, keep stillness inside of you." - Deepak Chopra

Okay!
Let me see if I can break this down for you in a way that is most effective, clear and enjoyable for you.

Apply what you learn here, thereby doing the research for yourself. As with everything - the proof is in the pudding, baby.

You gotta try it to determine.
Apply yourself to it.
Commit.
Do it all the way - for a time.

If you aren't going to do that, close this book now and give it away to someone you think might. Save yourself from wasting time reading some more "shelf help" (as the amazing Derek Rydall puts it).

I'm not here to fill your mind with something to feel cool about. I'm here to help you establish a practice that may save some of your lives, enhance your experience of life, and in the end assist humanity in awakening to living life in unbounded awareness, inner peace, passion, purpose, love and service.

There's a whole lot of badassery + fun to be had and I can not wait to explore that with you, people.

What to Do

I've already covered a myriad of ways that you can change your relationship with thought and witness all that can arise during a meditation practice.

I just want to reiterate a few things that I feel are worth stating over and over again as I have needed to hear them thousands of times.

Thoughts are a part of life and they will be a part of meditation. Thoughts are a part of life and they will be a part of your everyday experience.

You can change your relationship to thoughts by not thinking so much.

Thought comes and goes all by itself should you stay present enough.

Choosing to think while you're meditating is not meditating.

Having thoughts during meditation is just having thoughts.

If you notice yourself incessantly thinking with your eyes closed, it's no problem; it's just an old habit. Bring your attention back and see how devoted you can be to keeping your attention on your practice, allowing for the flow of spaciousness in between thoughts: thinking - practice - space - thoughts - thinking - practice - space.

You will get better and better at this to the point where there are far fewer instances of thinking. When you catch yourself having a thought, put attention right back on your meditative tool or on spaciousness.

Other Types of Experiences

Body Sensations
Sleepiness
Grogginess
Dream-like experiences
Falling Asleep
Crisp, Clear experiences
Exalted Metaphysical experiences
Light or Colors
Epiphany
Reliving of a Past Event
Memories
Thoughts of your to-do list
Thoughts of your fantasies and desires
Emotions
Emotions with stories attached
Rehashing past moments and what you or they could or should have done differently
Still silent peace - pure noticing with zero thought
And more

All of this is welcome - to be expected.
No type of experience is cooler than any other type.

We don't have an opinion of one type being less attractive than any other type.

Developing disinterest in which experience is presenting itself as soon as possible is liberating. In this way we develop interest in presence over the content of movement of the mind.

All of these types of experiences are a part of the movement of life. It all should be treated as secondary to the part of us observing them.They should all be treated as thoughts.

Thoughts should be treated as the meditation bell. A meditation bell reminds you to come present. It reminds you to put your attention on your meditative tool.

Therefore, whatever experience you realize that you are having is welcome and never more important than re-engaging your practice.

Discomfort

When discomfort arises during meditation, whether it is mental, emotional or physical, do your best to let it be.

Ask yourself, "Do I really need to get up right now? Do I really need to scratch that itch right now? Do I really need to move the body right now? Can I sit here for one more round of breath?"

This will help you to strengthen the muscle of discipline and deepen into your experience of meditation.

You are telling the mind that you are in control. That you will consciously be aware and present to your life now. You are choosing for your own presence to be at the forefront now rather than the unconscious streaming of the mind.

Emotion and Sensation

There are times when sensations and emotions can be overwhelming for us.

In the beginning we have the same relationship to emotions and some sensations that we do to our thoughts. We can change our relationship to them.

To change our relationship to them, we must give them the space to exist.

We must also pay so much attention that we do not identify with them creating stories around them. In my experience identifying with an emotion or a sensation in the body leads to a story which leads to exacerbated emotion or sensation which then leads to suffering.

I have personally changed my relationship to anxiety, fear, grief, sadness, anger, sexual energy, the sixth sense of empathy and beyond, by using this approach.

If you pay attention to the moment and allow for the energy of emotion or sensation to be present and move through as it will, you will no longer be bound by it, having the freedom to feel these emotions and sensations without them overwhelming you and running your life.

If you notice that anxiety for example is arising within you, look to see where the anxiety exists in your body.

Notice that the mind will want to label it as anxiety and will want to come up with a story about why it's there, why it's back and what it's going to do to you.

Instead put your attention completely on anxiety while resting back inside yourself: nowhere to go, nothing to label, nothing to decide about this particular energy.

If you can pay very close attention while remaining relaxed as can be in your body with the presence of anxiety bubbling up, you will stop yourself from the story that creates the overwhelm. This will stop the actual overwhelm of this particular energetic emotion.

I know that this may sound impossible and oversimplified. The mind doesn't value simplicity. Be willing to try anyway - because we are after all actively trying to change our relationship to the mind right?

I'm telling you from my experience that if you can practice giving all of your attention to resting back and letting emotion be there without commenting in your mind about it, you can change your relationship to it every time.

Play with this to the best of your ability. Explore playing with this exercise today.

Please come to the **Rock Your Mind Global** Facebook group and ask for any help you need with this particular exercise on any particular emotion or sensation that is troubling you.

I'd be more than happy to serve in assisting you in changing your relationship to any overwhelming emotion or body sensation that is getting in the way of your staying present to your life.

Now Let's Do This...

Basic Meditation Exercise

Get yourself settled into your meditation space and set your timer for the appropriate amount of time for practice.

Allow for yourself to settle into the space that you're sitting.

Take a few slow deep breaths, allowing for your body to relax from head to toe on every exhalation.

With every inhalation, allow for your awareness to expand - getting wide.

With every exhalation allow for your body to relax, held by gravity.

Recognize how much more alert you can become.

Feel the felt sense of gravity holding you where you are and let go of any muscle tension.

Awareness gets wider. The body relaxes.

Breathing Meditation

Right now with eyes open shift attention to the breath.

Just notice if you're on an inhalation or exhalation and watch the breath as it changes from an inhalation to an exhalation. Watch as the exhalation turns back into an inhalation.

Continue to allow for yourself to rest back - nowhere to go, nothing to do.

Give your attention completely to the inhalation and exhalation flowing as one continuous breath.

Notice how you don't have to do anything to make the breath come. It is unconditional.

The breath is unsolicited by you. It is gifted to you and through you by something greater than you.

Put more attention on the breath and if you become aware of anything else in your experience that's fine.

If more attention goes to a sensation or to a thought, simply bring all the attention back to the breath, watching as it turns from inhalation to exhalation and back again.

Gently close the eyes.
Let your awareness remain on or come back to the breath.
Watch the breath with restful alertness, for three rounds of breath, seeing if you can remain attentive without diversion.

Once you've observed the breath consistently for three rounds, you can move onto four and five and so on.

The goal is to be gentle with yourself as you exercise the muscle of remaining present.

Relax back in the body, attentive with the mind.

Watch the inhalation turn into an exhalation and back again.

See how many rounds of breath you can remain attentive without diversion.

Thoughts, feelings, sensations, noises may arise. They are welcome to.

Don't let any of it take your attention from the breath. Should any of these things become a diversion for you, taking attention away from the breath, it's no big deal. It's just an old habit.

You will get better and better at keeping your attention fixed on your meditative tool -- in this case the breath.

See if you can go for three rows of breath without diversion. If you can, continue onto the next breath until diversion occurs.

Once diversion occurs, hit the reset button and start from the first breath, again seeing how many breaths you can remain attentive.

It is best to have the attitude of curiosity here. How many rounds of breath can I have undiverted?

Continue this observation and flow through the length of time you have your timer set for.

Watch the breath. Watch the diversion. Come back to the breath. Repeat.

Bonus: Play with this shift of attention to breath in the midst of your day while in conversation, while in the midst of challenge, while in boredom, while in happiness - anytime. Notice what doing so does for your experience of life.

Mantras

You can choose a mantra that is in English or Sanskrit or whatever native language you speak.

Initially choose a Mantra that is one or two words - something that can flow with the breath.

For example:
Soham
Hamsa
Om Shanti
Om Namah

Peace Is
Be Still

Mantra with Breath

Choose your Mantra.

For the purposes of this illustrative instruction we will choose *Soham*.

Observe about 3 to 5 rounds of breath, undiverted.

Begin to implement your mantra.
On the inhalation think "so"
On the exhalation think "ham"
Continuing on for the length of your practice period.

When diversion occurs, let it be a reminder for you to come present again, giving full attention to breath and mantra like it is the first time, each time.

Guided Meditation

I want to make sure that you understand that I am an advocate or a cheerleader for you developing an effective meditation practice which will allow you to develop those higher states of consciousness and awesome personal self-mastery.

This outcome seems most consistent when one is sitting silently with oneself. However, to support yourself as you begin the journey, do what you gotta do!

You can utilize guided meditations from our FB live session in the group, from an app like Insight Timer, YouTube or any other resources to assist you in beginning the habit of consistent practice.

It may serve as training wheels to help you to feel more comfortable sitting still with yourself. Allowing for all of your senses to turn within during meditation is essential for the deepest level of healing and rewiring in your nervous system with no auditory stimulus.

There are times when people cannot get to that point. People who have too much stress healing all at once.

For example someone who is sick, recovering from a surgery, quitting an addiction, experiencing grief. These folks may most benefit from basic guided breathing exercises and not at all from meditation.

Many times this is helpful for people to feel safe enough to relax, heal and nourish their soul.

Level-Up Exercises

All of the following exercises were practices I either got from my teacher and lineage or are practices and prayers found out there for common consumption.

I do not claim any ownership rights to any of them. Each can be found in my facebook live transmissions.

I recommend trying them now as you are reading them. Implement immediately for best results.

Make a promise to yourself to begin using them on your own every day.

They are easy. You have access to them every single moment of your life.

Don't complicate this and don't toss it aside because of the conditioning that tells us that things need to be hard in order to be worth a damn.

Your life and your consciousness will change if you employ these practices.

Gravity

Just simply become aware right now with your eyes open; the gravity is holding your body right here.

Notice how you are holding yourself at attention with habitual muscle memory set points.

Completely let go into the felt sense of being held by gravity.

Now close your eyes and allow for yourself to give into that felt sense of gravity even further.

Relax your mind letting go of anything that you may need to do. There's nowhere to go there's nothing to do.

Give attention to how the body is held by gravity. Notice that your body doesn't need to hold itself up. Notice that your body doesn't need to stand at attention.

Just notice the gravity is always here.

Notice that you can put your attention on gravity in any given moment eyes closed or eyes open.

Notice the peace, the certainty, the support, the stability, the groundedness that comes from noticing how gravity is holding your body here in this very moment.

Open your eyes, continuing to notice gravity holding you here.

Begin to engage life, whether it be conversation or activity with this felt sense of being held.

Notice the difference in your engagement of life with that felt sense of being held by gravity. When in the midst of difficulty, boredom or even within an abundance of excitement, shift attention to gravity.

Notice how this changes your awareness of the spaciousness, the peace, the sense of rightness in your experience.

Noticing

Sitting comfortably with eyes open.
Notice the temperature in the room.
Notice the lighting.
Notice any noises.
Notice any sensations in the body.

Just allow.
Notice whatever you notice right now.

Closing your eyes.

Can you notice that the body is breathing?
Can you notice that you were held by gravity? Can you notice the back of your head?
Can you notice your right hand?

Can you notice the space surrounding you even with eyes closed?

Begin to just notice that you are here.
Be all here.
Can you notice that you exist?

Spaciousness

Sit with eyes open.
Allow awareness to get really wide.
(You may or may not experience this as your peripheral vision expands.)

Rest within, noticing all there is to be noticed. Notice the spaciousness that you yourself are sitting within. Notice the space that the environment exists within.

For example, if you are in a bedroom, notice the walls, the floor, ceiling and the contents of the room are existing within a certain amount of space.

If you are outdoors, notice the vast amount of spaciousness that exists appearing as air.

Notice that the entire earth, the entire solar system, the entire universe exists within space. Spaciousness is what all things are contained within.

You can bring attention to spaciousness within every atom. There is approximately 99.9% space in an atom.

Pure consciousness makes up a whole lot of what we perceive as matter. Spaciousness is truly abundant.

Play with this with eyes open in the midst of your day. Play with this with your eyes closed, watching for spaciousness even if you're using other tools.

Notice what paying attention to spaciousness does for your experience of life.

This is a great exercise when you're feeling overwhelmed, anxious or confused. At these times it is very soothing and restorative to shift attention to spaciousness, noticing just how much space there actually is.

Watching the Mind

Sit comfortably and maybe set a timer for 5 or 10 minutes.

Close your eyes.
Observe as the body relaxes.
Be held by the moment.

Notice if the breath changes.
Whether it does or not, after a few rounds of
breath, consciously engage the breath -
deepening it for one or two breaths.

No longer effort with the breath. Watch now.

Observe any self dialogue that comes
through the mind.

Observe any thoughts, your to-do list, any
thoughts of the past or the future that arise.

Notice if there is a tendency to be tempted to
talk back to these thoughts. Don't do that.

Refocus on breath or gravity. Then let
awareness be wide and just watch the
movement through the mind once again.

Keeping alert and attentive, notice without
labeling or analyzing.

Allow for whatever wants to come to come
and whatever wants to go to go without
attaching or identifying with any of it.

When anything captures your attention, come a little bit more present.

Watching the mind, observing in this way, will help you to recognize that you are this pure presence - witness to your entire life.

You will realize that you no longer need to identify with or attached to thoughts, feelings and circumstances.

You will begin to recognize fullness, aliveness, connection, purpose and happiness all emanating from your ability to simply watch the mind. This is because you will recognize that you are not now and never have been the movement of the mind but instead that which is in observance of the mind.

Prayerful Meditation Exercises

How to use this prayer in a meditative way... When you read the below prayer, make sure that you are settled or seated somewhere comfortably and that you bring your full presence.

If your mind begins to drift to some other moment or some other activity, bring it all the way back to right here right now. If you find that you've read a sentence of this prayer unconsciously, go back to where you remember reading last consciously and begin again.

As you read, feel into the essence of the words. This will be a very subtle thing and will require you to be relaxed and fully present.

You can also treat this as a contemplative prayer, considering how this prayer might be lived inside of your own life, what it means for you and to you if you were to be an instrument of peace living out the words of this prayer.

Be relaxed; be attentive; shift attention back at any point that you become unconscious and allow for the essence, the transmission, of these words to resonate to your bones, your cells, your DNA.

Do this in this way once a day for seven days and just take note of what the experience is like in your life as a result. Feel free to let us know in the Facebook group.

Prayer of Saint Francis of Asisi

Lord make me an instrument of Thy peace
Where there is hatred, let me sow love:
where there is injury, pardon:
where there is doubt, faith:
where there is despair, hope:
Where there is hatred, let me sow love: where
there is injury, pardon:
where there is doubt, faith: where there is
despair, hope:
where there is darkness, light; and where
there is sadness, joy.
Where there is darkness, light; and where
there is sadness, joy.
Oh Divine Master, grant that I may not so
much seek to be consoled as to console; to
be understood as to understand; to be loved
as to love.
For it is in giving that we receive; it is in
pardoning that we are pardoned; and it is in
dying that we are born to eternal life.
Amen

Serenity Prayer

God, grant me the Serenity
to accept the things I can not change,
the courage to change the things I can,
and the wisdom to know the difference.
Amen

3rd Step Prayer

God I offer myself to Thee
To build with me and to do with me as Thou
wilt. Relieve me of the bondage of self that I
may better do Thy will. Take away my
difficulties so that Victory over them may
bear witness to those I would help of Thy
Power, Thy Love and Thy Way of Life
May I do Thy will always.
Amen

Healing Meditative Practices

Ho'ponopono

Ho'ponopono is a Hawaiian prayer of reconciliation and forgiveness.

It allows you to clean up and heal your own mind, heart, body from carrying toxic experiences or from feeling guilty about something you are unable to make restitution for.

It doesn't have to feel good at first - especially if the person or situation you are calling in is downright ugly, traumatic and painful.

You should do this practice every day for at least 7 days, 2 or more times a day for at least 5 rounds..

Ideally, you will keep going each session until you find emotional release or peace beyond emotional release.

Likewise, you may continue this practice for longer than a week if you are not finding inner freedom and the blessing of healing coming from doing this practice.

It is very powerful if you truly give it your full attention and whole heart.

You can do this live with someone, hand on heart sitting face to face if possible. More often, it is used in quiet solitude.

- Sit quietly and come still inside.
- Call to mind the person or situation which there may be conflict with.
- Speak aloud or think these statements as if they are mantras or prayers and as if you truly mean it - even if they are initially difficult to feel.
- Repeat several times with full presence.

I'm sorry
Please forgive me
Thank you
I love you

Pink Light Technique

This practice is said to have come from the Rosicrucian line of teachings. It is used to heal pain and suffering. It is to be used daily and can be used with the same person or people each day or it can change.

● Move into a peaceful state. Deepen into that sense of being held by the Universe. Connect to either the felt sense of love right now, or remember a time when you felt completely loved.

● In your mind's eye, picture the pink light of unconditional love radiating from your heart and encompassing you. Imagine it like a pink sphere surrounding you.

● With a loving memory of yourself, bring to mind an image of you in another moment. This version of you stands outside of the pink light. In your mind's eye, picture yourself covering the new image of you with your pink light.

- Let the image go.

- Call to mind a loving image of a family member or friend - a time when they were happy and free. Cover them with your pink light. If more than one person shows up in your mind's eye, don't fight it - let them all show up, but cover each individually with pink light and let each of them go.

- Call to mind one you have discomfort with or even intense emotional charge with. Bring to mind a moment in time of them in their joyful perfection. Cover this person or these people with pink light and let them go.

- If you find it difficult to find a moment in your mind when anyone was happy and free, let an image of them as a child show up.

- Allow for anyone else to show up, following the same process above, remembering them happy and free, covering them with pink light and letting them go. In the beginning this process may take 10 minutes or so and eventually will get much faster.

If you aren't wired for visualization, no worries. Have your intent be unconditional love.

Once someone is done, assume that they are done for the day. Some people may show up again later or never again. Don't try to make them return.

Allow these people to come to mind from beyond your rational mind. No matter who shows up, and especially if there is resistance in you to do the Pink Light Technique, always do them anyway.

Remember to always do yourself first and daily.

Pineal Gland Technique

The pineal is the master gland.
Activating it helps regulate the hormones in the body and is extremely powerful for healing.

This technique takes about 15 minutes and should ONLY be done in the evening, preferably before bed. It can be done lying down or sitting up. It is said to be extremely useful for people with sleep disorders like insomnia.

- For the first five minutes:
    - Focus on your breathing. Each breath should be through the nose and all breathing should be done with the belly and not with the chest. Try to make each breath smoother and more even than the last. Spend the same amount of time on the in and out breath. Keep your breath connected, flowing, and smooth.

- For the second five minutes:
    - Keep the breath smooth and envision the inward portion of the breath entering the nostrils and lighting up the pineal gland in the center of the skull like an intensely bright light. Whether you actually see the bright light or not isn't important.

    - On the out breath envision that the pineal gland is sending the whole body what it needs to be healthy. If there is a specific issue that needs healing, you can focus the attention on just that part of the body.

- For the final five minutes:
  - Continue the same method for the in breath, but make a sound on the out breath.

  - At first this should be loud enough so you can hear it clearly, but with practice you can intone the sound quietly enough that someone sitting 15 feet away from you wouldn't be able to hear it.

  - There are different sounds you can use, depending on what needs healing.

  If you don't have any specific problems, use one of the sounds for your whole body like OM.

    - Whole Body: OOM, OM, AMEN, YAHWAY
    - Thymus and Upper Chest: EHM (pronounced aim)
    - Thyroid: MER (pronounced mir)
    - Sinuses: MMM
    - Chest+Heart: AH, MA
    - Throat: EYE (pronounced I)
    - Brain: EEE
    - Prostrate, Genital Areas: UH

- Lungs, Asthma: SSS
- Back Pain: WOOO

Nature Meditation

This exercise will deepen your relationship with the present moment, with intuition, with yourself as a part of the Universe and the Earth.

This exercise will help you change the habit of living only through the mind. It will give you access to a level of your own being that is covered up in the technology and the go-go-go of our modern world.

You will begin to develop a relationship with flow, synchronicity, magic, wonder, awe and innocence. You will begin to awaken the deeply connected part of you that is in kinship with Nature. You will feel more alive, grounded, carried and present.

- Find a place in nature that you can sit still for 10 to 30 minutes or longer if you like.

- Surrender to being potentially uncomfortable on the outside as well as internally settled in and comfortable. Welcome any bugs, weather, noises, sensations into the experience as part of this meditation.

- Begin by accessing your still, silent, center.

- Once you feel rested in witnessing consciousness, let your awareness get wide.

- Notice whatever is there to be noticed.

- Allow for everything to come and go exactly as it wants to, doing your best to keep the mind quiet. Do not allow yourself to begin to analyze or think about what you are experiencing.

- Drink in your surroundings.

- Bathe in the essence of this natural environment.

Expect that the mind will begin to move at some point.

Bring attention back to presence whenever the mind becomes active. If that feels difficult, become aware of the felt sense of being grounded and held by the earth, by gravity, by whatever you're sitting on and against.

When you have to recalibrate as the mind moves, don't waste any time being bothered by the fact that your attention was diverted. Instead immediately just allow yourself to relax into that felt sense and again.

Allow for awareness to get wide, shifting back into that witness state of consciousness. Again, noticing whatever is there to be noticed from this wide vantage point, bathing in nature.

Nature Meditation Level 2

The next level of this practice is choosing something in this natural environment to put your focus on. For example, you can choose to focus on a tree, a plant, an animal, the element of wind or the sun.

- Choose a focus object in your experience.
- Remaining rested back and held by gravity as you gently allow your attention to go to this one focus.

- Don't try to glean anything out of the experience. You are being present to it. There isn't a thing to understand. Simply observe.
- Bathe in awareness of and in a sense, listen with your whole body and whole being.
- The trick will be to not engage in any thoughts around what you are witnessing but to listen deeply.
- You may have to re-calibrate, shifting attention away from the mental movement and back to that felt sense of being held to awareness. Shift awareness back to the experience of witness consciousness. This diversion created by the mind is just a habit. It is no problem. It's to be expected and should be welcomed as a part of this meditation.

As you listen to whatever part of nature you're choosing to listen to, you may receive messages or epiphanies. This too is welcome but should be treated as another part of the movement of life and not held onto. Out of habit your mind will want to hold on to whatever revelations you're having. That's very normal. If you hold onto it, it will be at the expense of continuing to stay in a state of witnessing consciousness.

You can trust that whatever you are supposed to remember, you will remember when you are done with the meditation period. For convenience sake and to appease the mind, you could have a journal or a notebook handy with you for when you've completed this session so you can take notes of anything important that you wish to retain.

Gratitude Journal

Developing the ability to move into a state of gratitude is the key to experiencing abundance in this lifetime. Indeed gratitude unlocks our freedom.

Gratitude gives us access to recognizing all the good coming to us. When we are feeling defeated, like a victim, limited, challenged, or in any other way constricted, writing a gratitude list or journaling more deeply about the things we have to be grateful for is a powerful way to shift our vibration.

Shifting our attention to gratitude changes the trajectory of our life immediately. At least, that is my experience.

You may have had a gratitude list or journaling practice in the past. If so, you already have some ideas of where to begin.

If you've never heard of a gratitude list or a gratitude journal, it's very simple.

- Make a list of 5 to 10 things in your life right now that you can find to be grateful for.

- If that feels too simple for you, then begin to journal more deeply on those 5 to 10 subjects. Why are you grateful for them? How are you grateful for them? What blessings do they provide in your life?

- The next step of this gratitude exercise would be to express some of these gratitudes out loud to people who participate in making these blessings a reality in your life.

- You can also express them out loud on your social media sites, in an email, on the phone, in a text to your friends and family.

Notice what happens when you verbalize the things that you're feeling grateful for. This level of the gratitude exercise extends the blessing to other peoples' lives and overall expands consciousness and love in our world.

Don't take my word for that. Play with this. Watch the magic unfold for yourself.

Praise Exercise

Praise is simple appreciation.

There are times in our lives that feel so heavy it can be difficult for us to even find something to be grateful for.

We've all been there.

At such times, shifting attention to something in the environment that you can simply appreciate - like the clear blue sky - can open us to the upward spiraling currents in life.

Here's an example of praise in a common uncomfortable situation.

You are in a conversation with someone that you really don't like, someone who really rubs you the wrong way. You're having a very difficult time staying present. Your mind is dying for this to be over with, judging this person and totally checking out.

Here's what to do:

When it's your turn to talk, praise the person for something you genuinely appreciate about them.

It doesn't mean that you really are grateful for their existence in your life or that you really care for them. It simply is an acknowledgment of something that is true that you have access to in that moment. For example, you can compliment their eyes, their sweater, their jewelry.

Expressing praise out loud will shift the vibe of the conversation and possibly the dynamic of your relationship with this person.

Watch as you honestly express appreciation and how that breeds gratitude from that individual toward you.

Watch how that gratitude in turn expands the into a sense of connection that would have otherwise not been realized. Explore this and watch the results bless your life.

KeyPoints

★ Allow Allow Allow (best advice ever) Whatever is happening, let it happen. Don't waste a second on judging the experience of Meditation.

★ Not judging the experience also includes not judging some experiences as being better than others. Your mind will do so, but don't buy into it.

★ Thoughts, Emotions, Body Sensations - whatever arises should all be treated the same way. Like a thought. When you notice any of it, gently, with 100% attention return back to your meditation practice tool.

Quest Goals

★ Choose your type of practice if you don't already have one.

★ Close your eyes at least once today for 10-30 min (depending on your current level of practice. Be sure you are being realistic.)

★ When you notice you are paying attention to anything other than your practice tool, refocus.

★ Schedule in time to play with silent seated meditation as well as any one of the other practices in this chapter. Endeavor to get through them all!

★ Share your experience or ask for help in the **Rock Your Mind Global** Facebook group.

Worthy of Being Here for It All

Some part of me always knew it would be
true badassery to get to be here for *it all*.
To really be present to whatever You wanted
to present to me or inside of me.
The unflinching-from-the-core kind of
present. Open, vulnerable, innocent, in awe.
Not like the fake badassery that comes from
being an energetic steel door.
Not the kind that comes from the spiritual
facades of plenty I've often hidden behind.
The kind that a seasoned lover of *Yours* gets
to know.
It was brought to my attention that it was
identification with worth - and the
unworthiness it brings about.
Being fully present and surrendered to
staying right here I see that I have never
been touched or moved by a thing Except
Your Love.
So many notions have died in the dark, still,
silent experience of Your Holy Presence
within me.

Being Present

"Live quietly in the moment and see the beauty of all before you. The future will take care of itself...Forget the past, for it is gone from your domain!...Live supremely well now. This is the way of the wise."
- Paramahansa Yogananda

I just read a quote by Eckart Tolle - you know the famous author and speaker known for what it's like to live life in the present moment? This guy is one of very, very few in history who woke up into enlightenment just sitting there.

He was not meditating; he was not trying to attain anything spiritual in his life. He just woke up. This phenomenon is known as being hit by spiritual lightning.

Since he did not consciously traverse transcendence of the mind, he can not report to us how to get there. However, he beautifully describes to us what it is like inside of said living experience.

Here is the Tolle quote: "Realize deeply that the present moment is all you will ever have."

I had to go back and read it again.

My memory had it as: "You must deeply understand that this is the only present moment that there is."

Both point to an experience. How does that land in you?

I sat with the essence of these - basking in my own experience.

Eckart Tolle's shares often make me fall more in love with right now and increase the gratitude I have for my practice. There is gratitude and awe that nowadays I don't need to rely on Eckart or any of my other heroes or sheroes in consciousness to tell me what it's like - because I'm exploring it for myself.

At one point in this journey, I had read so many self-help books and heard enough stories of conscious awakening, to deeply believe that there was something more here. I realized one day that reading about it wasn't giving me an experience of it, however.

I threw a book across the room crying. "Enough hearing about these bastards and their awakened experiences. I want my own! How do I get my own?! When are they going to talk about that part?"

I discovered I had to stop feeding my mind and begin the work. The foundation of awakening is being present. Being present is being awake. Meditation is the most effective tool to deliver our attention to the present moment.

The present moment is always where our body is, where life is, but not so much where the mind tends to be.

Meditation re-conditions the mind to be here now. Right now is where life is happening. Right here and now is where you are.

You are not in the past. It doesn't exist. You are not in the future - it does not exist either.

Your body is right here. It cannot go to the past. It cannot go to the future. It can only be right here. Right?

See- you can even be logical about this, Rockers. Are you with me?

Right here, guys! Right here is where everything is. Everything you have longed for anyway. Everything of real value. Everything you have been taught to seek outside of yourself is here.

You have never left the present moment. Your body was always hanging out right here. It's been waiting for you to stick around long enough to remember where life really is happening.

It's been begging you to please be present, please stop stressing it out by trying to take it to the past or to the future all of the time. It's ready for you to knock that off already. It's been begging you to allow yourself to take a load off in this real-time moment.

Is THAT Rocking Your Mind yet, or what?

Just stop. Be here for a minute.

If you pay attention here long enough, you will discover that you never were separated from Universal Creative Intelligence. You never were separate from love or peace.

Your attention has been captivated by storylines of achievement and survival. Your attention has been conditioned to bounce around from comment to comment that your mind makes to itself. (Isn't that nutty?)

But YOU - the pure presence that is observing all of this - you never went anywhere. Isn't that INCREDIBLE????

Oh man. Just wait.

Having your mind ROCKED is FUN, but cultivating your own experience is way way better. You want that, right?

Vibe-Up Eyes Wide Open

You know that state when you are droning out - like when you are bored, tired, when it's hard to pay attention, etc...? That's when you need to vibe-up, people.

There are so many ways to do this: move the body, drink some water, change your breathing, close your eyes and meditate, or simply shift attention with eyes open to become more aware of the source of all energy, all creativity, all intelligence. Unplug from whatever is draining your battery, whatever is taking you down, and plug into your power source.

This is a very active practice and very different from what we are accustomed to. It is erroneously believed to be passive because we talk about the "being" aspect of this state. This is a misunderstanding.

We stop allowing the ego mind to run our attention all day long - thereby stressing out the nervous system and creating a life of lack, limitation, fear, crippling belief and habit, of unconsciousness. We begin to be present to what is. The mind quiets. We intuitively know what to do and where to go, how to live - engaged with the razor's edge of right now.

It is an incredibly active state - remaining attentive is very active, folks. It's just a very different kind of active than we are accustomed to.

In fact, let's look at this further.

We think we are being active because we are thinking, analyzing, conceptualizing, commenting to ourselves all day long. Nothing could be further from the truth.

So much of what we achieve from that state is autopilot, unconscious lazy dronery. It's easier to let life happen to us doing so-so work and feeling like a victim, taking very little to no responsibility for the quality of our presence, our work, our relationships, our lives.

In contrast, it is the highest degree of responsibility, love, consciousness to stay present to life.

Not judging what is coming through us, to us, circumstantially, emotionally, etc... is freeing. When one is fully present, there is no judgement - only awareness and fascination.

The mind may chime in that it doesn't like this, doesn't know what to do, doesn't understand, doesn't think this is right, doesn't feel good enough - but the mind's comments are so not compelling compared to the aliveness and fascination.

We choose to stay aligned with our true nature and full potential, with surrender to Holy Spirit Shakti flow and are simply curious to see what happens next.

Whenever we notice that we are not present, that we have gone unconscious, we make a conscious choice to Vibe-up by shifting our attention.

We go from a state of unconsciousness to a state of consciousness. This literally takes the Hz up several notches. Everything resonates at a certain frequency, made up of energy.

Everything is made up of consciousness, of the Creative Intelligence it came from. Everything has its own unique flavor and vibration - unique from every other part of the whole, while never being separate from that whole.

YOU have a unique vibrational essence. You have a certain frequency now that will refine and get stronger as you exercise the muscles of consciousness. You will begin to shine forth your true nature effortlessly in true badassery and those Hz will get higher.

You can't fabricate this. You can only practice it and allow it to unfold. When it blooms in you, you will attract different situations and people, teachers and peers, experiences of life which resonate at that higher frequency.

To speed that up or participate in it consciously, employ what you learn here. We literally vibe-up with our open-eyes consciousness practices, mindfulness, whatever works for you to shift your vibration, Om-ie.

Open eyes practice is essential in learning where you go unconscious and just simply shifting attention to be more conscious.

You Can Do This

You can be present because it's just shifting your attention -- and you can easily do that.

You are doing it unconsciously all day long with some moments of conscious engagement. You unconsciously allow it to run around, bounce around, identify, and assess this and that - wasting your life force energy, your creativity, your life.

You may not see this yet, but you will. Everyone is always shocked and sometimes (more often than not) horrified about how much this is, in fact, the way we live. When I say we here, I mean you - because it's no longer my experience.

Go ahead and let that irritate you if it does - then ask yourself - "who does she think she is?"

Just someone who's been shifting attention a shit-ton and continues to when I notice I am not giving full attention to inner stillness and silence. Then you might notice - "oh - she's not sharing this to brag, but to inspire me to find this experience for myself." BINGO.

But Hey! Forget my experience.
Go find your own.

Living in an awakened state is not hard, and it is accessible to most any human. I want you to know that and I dare you to employ the practices herein and beyond to find out. I deeply wish to serve you in developing awareness of and then -- quickly if you so choose -- intimacy with your own inner presence and with the present moment.

I dare you to be the one boldly and lovingly claiming your birthright and sharing it with others.

Please - Let go of the idea that everything has to be hard or it isn't worth a damn.

You are lucky.
Back when I consciously started this journey, things were clunkier and more dramatic. There were far fewer people on the planet exploring direct experience of consciousness than there are now.

There are a lot more conscious people on the planet now and more evolving into oneness consciousness than ever before. It has been birthing itself - this awakening.

Some of us were compelled; maybe even assigned, to show up consciously to the game before others. Others paved the way for me. Some of us have and do for you. You will, in turn, for those waiting for you to claim this true experiential awakening for yourself.

Yeah, that's right.

Those behind you are waiting. They can't do it until you do. It's like waiting in line to go potty - so get on with this already, hey? If you won't commit for you, for goodness sake help those poor souls out waiting on you!

You CAN learn to sit silently in meditation, and you CAN learn how to be present. You may have had the wrong tools, the wrong information about how to use the tools, the wrong idea about what being present is, what the purpose of meditation or even of what being present is - and all of that is common and fixable. Are you open to that?

Are you open to what you think is true being wrong or at least not the full picture? Are you open to this journey of being present, of evolution into higher states of consciousness being possible? Are you open to it being a simple, fairly easy journey if you follow some experienced guidance here on this epic adventure?

Clarity and confidence seem to require experienced guidance. At least, that is what I have seen in folks for the last few decades. This is definitely my experience. I needed and still need my teacher.

Great news! I believe this book can assist you in becoming clear and confident with both meditation and being present.

As with all else, you have to employ what is shared and consistently so as you proceed with this Adventure. I guarantee that if you do, you will get an excellent foundation as well as guidance on how to keep going.

Mindset will make you or break you as we attempt to level-up here. A success mindset includes expectation that you will see doubt, fear, and your unique habits of unconsciousness.

A success mindset also includes accepting these habits as they arise. Choosing to look at them as the Universe's meditation bell bringing you back to the moment - or to your practice.

Success includes being present enough to see what has been unconscious, welcome it as a reminder to employ your new habits of coming present, and to keep going.

You must be open to not knowing anything but to seeing everything. You must be innocent, curious and willing to implement immediately. You have to see the ways you do not believe this is possible. You must know what your mind likes to come up with to derail you. You must be honest about it and willing to find a different experience.

If you say you have no doubts, I will challenge you. The mind always doubts it can stay present and conversely will talk to you about how well it's doing staying present.

The mind will inevitably dislike the idea of meditating at some point and will arrogantly determine it doesn't need help anyway. What are you going to do when these moments arise?

Employ your practice immediately. In doing so you change neurology, physiology, your normal mode of operation, and you create a new mode of operation. In doing so, you protect your most prized asset - your evolution into conscious badassery.

Exercise

Stop. Take this moment right now. Be all here. Consider: Where do you see that your mind convinces you that you don't need to follow through at some point in life?

Take a look at the moments of your life where you shrank back into comfort instead of leaning into the edge of aliveness. You know - moments of self-sabotage.

What compelling story did you pay attention to in your mind during these times.

Sit still long enough to really let yourself see what unconsciously goes on at these times.

Go tell us what you discovered from this inquiry and what is up for you right now in the **Rock Your Mind Global** Facebook group.

You have to see it and know how to win in those moments, or you will return to the drone state and believe that this didn't work for you.

You can choose to let a voice in your head win, and it won't be long before life is back to the compromise of a crushed soul resigned to it being good enough.

Some of you will even make that my fault because that is your unique habit. It was one of mine, telling myself things like, " Oh, it didn't work for me because she didn't really resonate for me." When really I did not give it 100%.

What level of self-respect do you imagine people have at that point?
You are meant for more.

If you choose to half - ass this, those are the results you will get. You will never attain full human consciousness. You will not attain the level of badassery - not ever - that is possible for you.

Do this thing though, keep going, employ every Quest you get, continue to follow suggestions, and eventually it will dawn within you and pour forth from you, blessing this world.

Your divine badassery will radiate forth, serving others just in your aliveness. That's what I'm talking about.

Being Present

The qualities of being present include: no sense of time or space, no sense of yourself, no sense of needing anything to be different - just pure experiencing what is. A sense of anything needing to be changed about the moment is non-existent.

In other words, there's no commenting on the moment, no mental chatter robbing us of the purity of it, and so it is experienced as perfect - though that may not be a conscious thought.

The best moment of your life, the peak moments you have stumbled into, have had these qualities but also intensity. These moments of our lives feel big. This has led to an erroneous assumption that when we wake up, when we are present, that things will never be challenging, never feel bad, never be disliked by the mind and will be glamorous.

We believe that it will be big all the time and that bigness is what happiness is (at least, if you are wired like me.) Of course that isn't the deal.

Further we believe that it isn't possible to be present to life and transcend the rollercoaster. To the shut down heart and to the rigid mind: this is hogwash, non-sense, unattainable. " *I mean, maybe this is attainable by Jesus or Buddha - but give me a break.* "

You aren't one of these rigid doubters, though, are you? Nah - you can't be. I mean, there may be resistance and fear that arise. There may be some degree of mental skepticism. That's fine.

Anyway, being present is not about belief. It is about an experience.

Can you feel into having even 25% or 50% of what these awakened beings are said to have had?

Well, my people, you can tap into and stabilize that living experience. As you practice being present, it becomes more and more obvious, familiar, stable, clear.

Being present becomes more the baseline experience - as opposed to the following of thoughts and emotions out into the drone-like state of the average human.

You become awake to all of life. There is a zest in the mundane and a peace in the intense. Resistance and grasping dissolve. There is grace.

Passionate aliveness and a complete unwavering devotion to, communion with, and commitment to discovering more pure presence and life lived in the present moment becomes the norm.

Not only for a chosen few, not only for folks like me who decided to go do all kinds of training, become a monk and such.
For you.

And it's about time we start manifesting that as our new credo, narrative, norm.
You feel me? You down?
YES!!!

How to Practice Being Present

So how do we attain this?
Shifting attention of course. Shifting and focusing attention. You're going to get really good at that.

You are going to get really good at replacing the old habit of unconsciousness with consciousness. You are going to wake up from the drone state on the path of badassery, my Om-ie.

The potential in you emerges and unfurls so effortlessly when you are out of the way. Living in the moment and being present to life is so simple it's ridiculous.

This Quest requires a good why or purpose - your personal mission. Remember that one? Why are you here?

That heart's greatest desire is very important to be clear about. If you don't have a clear one yet, or it isn't truly captivating to your innermost self, let us know in the **Rock Your Mind Global** Facebook group so we can assist you in finding it. You will need to be in touch with it throughout life.

You'll also need continual support, encouragement, and guidance. Hurrah!

We are Questing together here in this cosmic sandbox! This Questing requires a bit of grit and definite devotion on your part to keep going. So let's play with that inner Jedi emergence, shall we?

Engage. Be playful. Enjoy!

Tips for Being Present

In order to practice being present, a plan is useful. Allow me to offer up some proven effective tips for your plan!

Desire

First thing you need to know is that your desire brought you here and this is part of your WHY. So keep feeding it, sharing it, and whatever it takes to remember it at the forefront each day. Write it down, print it out, use images on an altar or your bathroom mirror. Why do you care to be present to your life?

The Present Moment Lightswitch

Second, you should not over-complicate this journey. There's no middle area: you either are being present or you are not. The lightswitch is flipped on or it is off.

Not Wasting Time on Unconsciousness

Thirdly you should know that in one moment you can be unconscious and the next you can be present. No need to waste time wondering why you were just unconscious or why you can't stay present.

Give all attention to being as present as you can. Eventually you will grow the muscle of maintaining present moment awareness through the use of your tools.

At certain points you will see how you go unconscious and you will be able to come back sooner, or even stop yourself from drifting when it starts.

Exercise

Don't do a thing.
Just rest here.
Be present.

See... You know how to do it.

The mind will always want to overcomplicate
this. Don't do it.
Notice the space surrounding you.
Don't label anything.
Don't consider anything.
Don't care about any movement or any
contents in your space, nor in your mind.

What's this like - just resting here? What's
this like, being held by gravity... by the
moment? Is there spaciousness? Is there any
degree of peace?

Avoid any attraction to close your eyes. Keep
them open and allow.

Allow for your awareness to get wider.

There is nowhere to go. There is nothing to do. Just rest attentive.

Feel that felt sense of being held by gravity.
Let attention remain wide.
Notice when the mind wants to hone in on any element and begin to chatter about it.
Rest back.
Breathe.
Nothing to figure out or achieve.
No goal to attain.
Witness.
Not trying to retain anything.
Held by gravity. Awareness wide.
Can you notice your own presence?
Can you notice that you exist?
What's this part of you like?
Still? Silent? Purely Aware? Peaceful?
Beautiful. Well done.

Remain rested inward and proceed with life from here. What a sacred gift.

Contemplative Exercise

Would you say that remaining present to each moment of your life is pretty Badass?

How many moments of your life are you present to?

How many moments are not thinking your way through it?

How many moments is the voice in your head commenting on everything?

How many moments is the mind quiet?

How do you know that you are being present?

Questing Bonus: Spend half a day (set reminders to go off throughout the day) and observe: How often are you so present that you are completely engrossed in life with a quiet mind and relaxed body?

Signposts Throughout the Day

Past or Future Thoughts

Anytime you are noticing that you are wrapped up in the past or future thoughts, relax the body, notice gravity, put attention on breath, then let awareness come wide. Completely disengage the mental dialog and become fully attentive to getting into present moment state.

Conflict + Challenge

It is very easy to use conflict and challenge in our lives as reminders to be present because we don't like these experiences. Often we tune out as a subtle way of pushing away these experiences, but these moments can be awesome opportunities to exercise the muscle of being present.

It's best if you set yourself up at the start for not pushing these experiences away at all, but in recognizing that you are shifting attention to gravity, spaciousness, the breath, a mantra, in order to be present to what is, rather than to run from it.

It's awesome that uncomfortable circumstances or thoughts can provide contrast and incentive to come more present to your precious life. You also will get to find out what a badass you can be - keeping present in the midst of discomfort.

True Listening

Whenever you notice yourself anticipating what to say within a conversation, bring attention to that felt sense of being held by gravity. Allow yourself to give all of your attention to that and listen from here.

Your mind can not figure this out. Don't bother wasting energy.

Go try it right now.
If gravity doesn't work for you, put all attention on spaciousness, the breath or even a mantra - and listen while doing this. The mind won't like it at first.

Then quickly you'll feel like a Jedi-Ninja because you'll stop trying to prove points, stop exhausting yourself with being clever and being right, and you will start to hear what the other person's heart is trying to convey. You will begin to really listen and hold space in a way you may never have done before.

You will bless your nervous system and other people's lives. People will notice. It may be confusing, scary or compelling to them in some way.

You will see the proof is in this pudding as soon as you start playing with it.

You will have questions - go share them in the group.

A Sense that there is Something Wrong

When should you practice this?
You should practice this anytime you notice that you are not being fully present.

Not being present includes a sense that there's just *something wrong* with me or this moment or the circumstance that I don't know how to fix.

It might include a sense that there is *something missing* or just *not quite right*.

It might include full-on fantasizing about the future at the expense of the present without solid objectives to take you toward your goals and vision.

All of these should be sign posts for you to just shift attention to breath, gravity, spaciousness, your mantra - whatever tool you're using to be present.

While these techniques may seem like anybody would have made them up and so simple that you don't know why you invested in this book in order to get this information, I assure you that you need to employ it consistently and get feedback on how it's going for you.

Otherwise, you are going to just put this in the conceptual space in your head and your life will not change. You will not change your relationship to thought; you will not change your relationship to the limitations you are identified with; you will not change your relationship to the magnificence that is emerging or wanting to emerge through you; you will not live inside of higher states of consciousness badassery.

Reminders

Why do we practice these exercises, techniques, or meditation?

We do this to unplug from stress, to protect from stress, to unplug from the incessant hammering of the mind, to interrupt the habit of being unconscious and not being present to life.

We do this to plug into the source of energy, creativity, aliveness, passion, love, peace, and purpose. The basic, fundamental practices and principles which have been taught to me over the last two decades I have needed to hear and implement with innocence.

I have needed to receive them as though I have never heard them before. Bear in mind, it is basic, rudimentary, fundamental practice and principle that everything else is based upon. Further refinement, deepening and expanding can only come from mastery of the basics.

KeyPoints

★   The Present Moment is all you will ever be living inside of - all you will ever have.

★   Life happens where your body is.

★   You can train yourself to be present.

★   We all lived in the present moment as children - so your body remembers what that state is like and longs for it.

★   Droning out is an awesome reminder to come present again.

★   Thinking about the past or future can be great reminders to come present again.

★   Becoming present again can be done in many simple ways that are with you all of the time - they only require you to actually do them.

★   Being present ultimately is a shift of attention. Since attention naturally moves all day long, this is simple. You do it unconsciously but you will begin to do so consciously now.

★ The qualities of being present can be experienced but can not be replicated by the mind.

★ Knowing how being present affects your nervous system and life will be helpful for you to determine a personal "why" for committing to this practice. Having a "why" will keep you playful and determined to keep going.

★ You want to be present. You've been unconsciously longing for and seeking this your whole life. Your body and world need you to be present.

Quest Goals

★ Close your eyes for 5 or 10 minutes more than usual.
★ Practice the consciousness exercises in this chapter.
★ What did you discover from the Noticing Exercise?

★ What did you discover from the Questing Bonus after the Noticing Exercise?

★ Share your experiences in the **Rock Your Mind Global** Facebook group.

Supreme One

The multitudes beckon attention - almost
every one leads me to suffering. Endless
seeking, bettering, advancing, growth.
Endless attempts to connect.

Only YOU deliver me into sanity. Into
freedom. With You, everything else that
distracted me in endless circles can be met in
awe as a piece of Heaven.
The difference is stark, crisp, magnificent.
With attention on the multitudes, there is the
appearance of the many and separation.
With attention on YOU - I awake to realize
the ultimate reality. There is just One.
This is the ultimate "connection." Though in
this stable, steady reality, connection isn't a
thing. Connection suggests that there is
more than one thing - and there is not. You
have set me free. I am no longer identified as
a drop of this ocean, but righted in
perspective, identified as the Ocean itself.

PART FOUR

THE SACRED PAUSE

The Sacred Pause

"Be Still and Know" - Jesus

It's such a powerful thing to be so present that you notice, yet do not comment to yourself in your head on what you are noticing. Pristine. Pure. Absolute. Unadulterated.

In noticing, you will see everything. You'll begin to notice what you did not know was lurking about, running your life in unconscious ways.

You will also notice all the magic and love that has been hiding out in you, trapped by habitual repression.

What the average human does is ignore. Unconsciously of course. As one evolves and is pushed by typically painful circumstances to grow, one will have to look at and begin to take responsibility for what is going on. This becomes either a chore or an exciting adventure.

As my teacher tells me - "good - see everything." I didn't want to see what I suspected to be true, because I was under the mistaken impression that there was a lifetime of work to be done before I was ever worthy to rest in peace and experience passionate aliveness.

What has been revealed to me is that while it may be a lifelong adventure of expanding awareness and discovery, of growth, it is not at the expense of knowing peace or passionate aliveness now. Both growth and peace co-exist. Rest assured.

Most humans believe that peace is in some other moment. We believe that we will know peace when we have worked on issues enough so that nothing unconscious is running.

We believe when we are fixed, healed, awake enough, circumstances are never challenging and therefore we will know peace. We believe that when there is no longer anything that is scary for us, we will know peace.

Oh to see this lie unravel! It is incredibly delightful to discover that I can only know peace in becoming aware of it, clear about it, prioritizing the practices and circumstances that fortify and anchor it, protect the experience of it - no matter what is happening inside or outside of me. What a huge shift in perspective.

It can not ever happen from the outside in and last. It can only happen from the inside out. It is only possible to attain that peace of mind and freedom when I am actively willing to allow all things to be as they are and choose peace anyway.

It is absolutely crucial that we accept responsibility for our lives in this way. I find that I can not transcend a thing unless I am willing to stay present to it, allow it, and thereby give myself the capacity to change my relationship to it.

Having said this, I find very little attention needs to be on fixing or changing what I see isn't working. I find that making the infinitely still, silent presence within more important than an identification with a puny little issue has massive impact in terms of changing my life for the better. This takes practice.

It has also required a lot of reminding and redirecting from my own teacher. We can not rise into full human consciousness without welcoming the shadow parts of us, "personally" or collectively.

Everything must be met with quiet presence to be seen for what it is - God/consciousness, or nothing at all.

There is a strange idea in the spiritual world that suggests we are doing well and on-to-something if there are no bumps in the road. When one is fully present, the appearance of bumps has no effect on the witness. The witnessing presence is unmoved, unrocked, unshakeable.

But look, it is still a part of life and growth to take a look at things and recalibrate accordingly. Best to be matter of fact and not emotional about this.

Just do it, ya know?
Let us assess...

Where are You?

We are somewhere inside of this 21 Day Journey. Do you need to recalibrate?

Now, take a moment to get your journal or notebook, or open a fresh document and get to sharing the facts.

Below you'll find many questions to help you take an honest assessment. Take a look and work with what makes most sense for you in your life right now.

Don't dramatize this. If you have a habit of being hard on yourself, don't waste a moment whipping yourself if you aren't where you think you should be.

Honestly - don't waste your time. Don't make it worse than it is.

Don't be in fantasy land about it either. What has in fact been happening?

Then, if necessary hit the reset button and make those pivots in how you are showing up. Or, if you are keeping steady here, look at how you might spice it up and step up your game. I love doing both of these things every month or so.

Contemplation Exercise

What was your original plan?
Was it a realistic plan?
Are you keeping on task reading and implementing the practices and quest goals?

Are you keeping your practice time sacred, untouched, never abandoned for the sake of your partner, our children, your comfort zone?

Are you connecting in the Rock Your Mind Global Facebook group?

Do you still have your reading, practice times, check in times all scheduled in your planner, calendar, etc...?

Do you still have Reminders set? Do you need to go fill those in right now and reset them?

Do you need to go check in on FB and with your accountability partner or team?

Where are you compromising on what you say you really want? Where are you not prioritizing it?

Have you been compromising on how many times a day you are closing your eyes or are you increasing the number of times you close eyes? Are you getting longer sessions or shorter sessions in?

Are you remembering to engage with eyes open as often? How are you keeping yourself playful and connected?

What is and isn't working? What worked before that you need to get back on board to protect and sanctify this holy mission of yours?

Did you forget your Why? Do you need to reset your mindset? What brought you here? Did life get better and then you decided you didn't need to do this anymore? Deepen back into why you are showing up.

Where do you intend or even plan and then abandon your dream, your health, your goal, your peace to make someone else comfortable, for you to be less inconvenienced, to go with the status quo or to not have to be uncomfortable yourself?

Where do you schedule and then not protect your sacred adventure into awakening?

Where do you forget your "why" over and over again? Where do you hold yourself accountable? Where won't you compromise? Where are you succeeding at staying with yourself and your deepest desire? Where are you crushing it?

Do you need reminders about the Science of meditation and being present?

Do you need reminders about what that bigger purpose or perspective may be in your practice and evolution?

Read on, look up inspiration to continue on YouTube, seek out other sources, do what it takes. (but also, get your dang eyes closed)

Your Why

Are you in touch with your Why? Has it shifted? Do you need to reconnect to it? What is it now?

Schedule + Protect

Where are you at with getting in practice (eyes closed and opened), reading, fb group check ins and any other accountability check ins scheduled? How are you prioritizing them? How are you protecting the schedule? How can you uplevel here?

Be realistic. Be honest.

Meditating

Are you getting your eyes closed? The amount you intended? How many times a day? For how long each session?

Are you holding yourself accountable with the group, a partner, logging in to Insight Timer or other? Are you feeling clear about what you are doing? Have you taken advantage of the other resources on the planet, your own personal teacher, or stopped in for one of the FB live classes in our group?

What do you need to reset, keep going, go deeper?

If you aren't' getting practice in, is it because you are too busy, aren't' protecting your peace, are you feeling confident, or confused?

Do you still doubt what you are supposed to be doing in there with eyes closed? What can you do to support yourself?

Eyes Open Practices

Are you setting reminders and actually shifting attention with each quest goal suggestion?

Are you playing with this and sharing what you discover?

Have you shared in the fb group what you are finding, questions, confused about, celebrating? How can you set yourself up for success and step up your game here?

Rock Your Mind Global Facebook Group

Have you joined?
Have you introduced yourself?
Have you continued to check in and share?
Have you bonded with another member?

Are you being vulnerable?
Are you asking for help?
Are you showing up to the live classes?
If not, why not?

If you were but haven't been lately, hit the reset button. Time to level-up.

Quest Goals

Are you implementing these immediately?
Picking and choosing?
Half-assing the implementation or going all in to really see if you can get the results shared here? Why or why not?

What are you enjoying about employing these Quest Goals? Are you sharing your results with family, friends, community, the fb group? Why or why not?

When you have implemented the Quest Goals what has that felt like? What did you notice?

When you skip over it, what was the result?

Are you ready to level up? What will that look like for you?

Support

Are you getting support?
Do you have others joining you in this adventure?

If not, consider rebeginning and getting a study/practice group together.

Are you asking for help in the fb group? Have you used any meditation apps, purchased any programs or attended any of the live Facebook classes or watched them after the fact?

Have you joined any live groups in your area?

Have you considered other forms of support such as a training or coaching program?

What are you doing? What aren't you doing? What are you drawn to do that you haven't done yet? What can you do now?

Reading the Book

Obviously, you are reading this book right here and now. You may have flipped it open here or skimmed to this part, or even read your way here.

If you've read from the beginning, how long did it take you? Are you on track with your original date goal? Can you hit the reset button and set a new date if need be?

How often are you setting aside to consciously engage this book and the adventure it suggests?

Do you have time scheduled on your calendar for reading this book? Are you willing to start scheduling it now if you are falling short of your goal or even just as an experiment to see if it has any positive impact or not?

What else can you do to support yourself in getting through this book in a timely manner?

Have you shared this adventure with others? That can be a huge inspiration for following through.

KeyPoints

★ The Sacred Pause is a thing life provides us with, but we can and should also consider gifting ourselves with this experience each day in Meditation and in a separate time to contemplate our success of growth and how we'd like to become more aware, how to vibe-up and level-up in our practice and life. Make time for the Sacred Pause.

Questing Goals

★ Consider each question in this chapter and hit the reset button as needed.

★ Then keep going, you badass Adventurer, you!

The Rhythm of the Sacred Pause

I have sat still just enough to recognize Her
lulling force of Rhythm.
I begin to become capable of recognizing
Her ways. She is unstoppable, predictable,
unpredictable. She flows and ebbs - she
pauses.
I begin to attune to Her more readily, a bit
more steadily. She teaches me patience,
stillness, presence.
She reveals Rhythm in this body each day.
She reveals Her cycling with the moon and
Her seasonal dances with Gaia and the Sun.
She reveals Herself to me in the Rhythm of
the day rolling into night and in the inhale
and exhale of these lungs.
She shows Herself to me cycles of life, death,
rebirth. She shows me Herself in the cosmic
birthing of consciousness.
I am initiated in giving Her my attention. She
impresses upon me the medicine of the
Sacred Pause - how to choose it as well as
accept the unexpected pausing.
She offers me the deep wisdom of this pause,
surrendering to Her here gifts me with that
which I yearn for.

PART FIVE

EMBODIMENT OF BADASSERY

Badass States of Consciousness

"Energy, like you, has no beginning and no end. It is only ever shifting states."
- Panache Desai
"No problem can be solved from the same level of consciousness that created it." -
Albert Einstein

If he's right (Einstein), and he seems to be, then there must then be another level of consciousness into which we can develop as our new setpoint.

I was conditioned by our societal norms to accept and live into humanity's current limiting beliefs and underlying narrative about how being a human means being identified as a body, a personality, a collection of beliefs about myself, circumstances and my world.

I heard about things like a *soul* which seemed to be more in touch with the divine perhaps - but I also heard that my soul *needed saving*. That was confusing.

No one ever told me about consciousness. No one ever said, "you are that which is aware of the body, the thoughts, the personality, the world." No one knew about it around me, so how could they?

I was led to believe that enlightenment only happened for Ninjas in far off lands, Jedis in Sci-fi movies, Hindu renunciates in the Himalayan caves, people who existed several thousand years ago like Buddha and Jesus - but not for folks like you and me.

I was trained to habitually seek in the mind for a better way, an improved way, a way out, a way through - using the same level of the mind that created the current reality.

At some point I realized that we've all been habituated to live inside of mental commentary, analyzing moment to moment rather than experiencing life purely. I also began to notice that we all intuit that there is *something more*...

Einstein: *Still, there are moments when one feels free from one's own identification with human limitations and inadequacies. At such moments, one imagines that one stands on some spot on a small planet, gazing in amazement at the cold yet profoundly moving beauty of the eternal; the unfathomable: life and death flow into one and there is no evolution nor destiny, only being.*

You've had these moments. Maybe often. Maybe only once that you can recall.

Remember?

Humans were born with the ability to be super present to life. The senses were fascinating. The body was fascinating. The circumstances of life were fascinating. Nature was extremely fascinating. The dynamics around us between other humans were fascinating.

We didn't even know we were human. We did not experience identification with thoughts because we actually had none - everything was simply intuitive knowing.

Eventually imprints of repeated experiences forged identification - with limitation, separation and unconsciousness.

My oldest daughter and I continued to talk about her own consciousness until she was about 8. I would encourage her to put her attention on the still, silent part of her. She was very aware and familiar with it.

Around age 8 she told me it was getting hard to stay present - aware of "the peace" - that everyone around her was falling asleep and it was easier for her to fall asleep too. That moment brought me to my knees - the part of me that didn't want her to take that path.

The bigger part of me knew that she had to - that this decision and choice was conscious for her, unlike many of us. I made the same choice. We all made the choice.

It has been suggested by Yogic Science lineages that we make this choice in order to remember. Meaning, we identify with limitation so that we can return to the state of remembrance. Like a game.

This notion has always deeply resonated with me. I believe that there may come a time in humanity's evolution when people remain awake - that falling asleep doesn't have to happen any more. I believe it just isn't that point in the divine play yet.

Yet after watching this play out for several decades, it appears that we grow ever-closer to a reality where all humans have evolved into higher states of consciousness. It has been documented both in ancient traditions and in modern Sciences that keeping present leads to some really cool superhuman badassery.

For example, true miracle healing, intuitive understandings of one another and the world around us, vitality and longevity of the nervous system, and the blissful expression of life through us. I have been witness to the evolution in me and around me.

Science has shown it is so. Ancient prophecy says it is and will be so. In you right now it is so. Until that full expression anchors in humanity, the awakening continues.

Exercising the muscle until it remains strong and is sustained is what we get playfully to explore.

States of Consciousness

What is a State of Consciousness?

Consciousness is a widely explored and yet still somewhat mysterious element of human life. It is the basis of our awareness of ourselves and life.

The 99.9% space that is found in every atom is said to be consciousness. Science has just had a hard time explaining it. Science has, however, described it as the Quantum Field.

The Quantum Field is said to be conscious, responsive, and interactive. The Quantum Field is the backdrop of all that arises. It is suggested that the Quantum Field is the thing that all particles appear within, exist within, express within, die within.

Because all modern-world humans have been conditioned to identify with the .1% that appears to be solid matter, as well as identified with all the content flowing through the Quantum Field (rather than with Consciousness itself) we are a bit clueless.

Given just a bit of time returning awareness within, we sense that we are home and all manner of intuitive magic and blessings unfurl as a result. Including, re-establishing life in the present moment.

Living in the present moment is not at all the same state as the typical waking state most of humanity has been in.

What are the Primary States of Consciousness?

States of consciousness are scientifically measured and distinguished from one another by comparing brain activity and physical rest.

The typical human lives cycling through 3 relative states of consciousness daily. The 3 relative states of consciousness include waking, dreaming and the dreamless sleep state.

In the waking state, there is much brain activity, albeit often incoherent and chaotic. The body is up moving around and the mind is alert.

In the dreamless sleep state (non-REM) the body is in absolute rest and the mind is not at all alert.

In the dreaming (REM state) the body is not in absolute rest as stress is healing and emotional/physical digestion may be taking place in the mind and body, yet the mind is also not alert to the outside world in this state.

Other States of Consciousness

There are altered states of consciousness that we are familiar with achieved through drug use, including marijuana and hallucinogens, alcohol use and traumatic experiences.

The meditative state is often considered another altered state of consciousness - albeit a truly natural one induced by simply shifting attention and developing focus.

In the meditative state, the mind is alert and in complete coherence and the body is at rest. This is a very unique state from the 3 relative states and the most ideal state for developing higher states of consciousness.

Oftentimes folks fall into a deep meditative state without proper tools to consistently take attention back and tether it in there.

When one does have effective tools, the charm of resting in that still, silent conscious presence is magnetic and clear. It becomes easier to identify and "drop into" at will.

This ease and clarity makes returning to and sticking around in this state easier and easier with eyes closed.

This experience will bleed out into daily life of course, but it does so more effectively and completely if one has a proper tool for accessing this state - consciously communing with it by turning attention back toward it throughout the day with eyes open, as we have discussed.

There is a difference between tapping into a state and living effortlessly inside of it like we do with the 3 relative states. When it becomes a clear experience with eyes opened and closed this becomes a new setpoint for that nervous system - enter the 4th state of consciousness.

With eyes open we have randomly tapped into that state as well - witnessing something beautiful, soul-stirring, running a marathon, rocking out on stage. Abraham Maslow called this phenomenon "peak experience."

Some part of us knows that if we can tap into this experience by chance, then we can arrive there again by will. People chase after this experience in so many ways.

There is only one way to enliven that state consistently. We do not do so by trying to recreate the exact same external circumstances. We don't do it by learning about it and analyzing it in our mind. We establish this by way of consciousness.

The 4th State

The 4th state has been called many things around the world. It is known as Turiya, Samadhi, Satori, and the peace that passeth understanding. It is a measurable state by an eeg machine.

Someone in this state would show consistently coherent brain waves - not just in meditation. In this state there would be the presence of more dopamine, serotonin and oxytocin in the bloodstream than adrenaline and cortisol throughout the day.

A nervous system in this state would continue to be in meditation regularly as well as practicing being very present all of the time.

It is of highest probability that this nervous system has been guided and supported into this state of consciousness by someone who has previously walked the path of awakening successfully. Without guidance one invariably relies on the mind, and winds up back in a state of dronery rather than staying still in wakefulness.

The fourth state allows for the protein molecules in your body to stick around without being fought off by the stress hormones. When these molecules hang out long enough, they are nourished, fortified and morphed into even more beneficial molecules of longevity, vitality and wellness.

These beneficial molecules are why yogis and meditators tend to look etheric, eternally youthful, glowing. It's a thing that cannot be fabricated - just like your vibes.

Over time, the peace that passeth understanding is so obvious that one becomes compelled by the universal magnet to stay and stay and just keep staying present.

Beyond the 4th

Beyond the 4th state is a state often known as one of "praying without ceasing," Nirvakalpa Samadhi, Cosmic Consciousness, or Enlightenment.

Don't let those words and their associated concepts fool you or concern you. Labels are nothing other than ways for us to attempt to communicate experience. Experience is everything. Your Experience is EVERYTHING.

This becomes yet another state where, at any given moment it is clear that you are engaged in the greatest love affair of all. Nothing has more of your attention than this. You are aware of everything that comes through and to you but are not identified with any of it.

You resist no circumstance. You wouldn't dream of resistance because it would shatter the state that has become more alive than anything of this world. Ironically - this world becomes exceedingly more alive, magical and awe-inspiring (including the body/mind you inhabit). You marvel at how real it seems, yet how clearly unreal it is.

This can not be understood by your current state of mind, friend. Let it pull you forward but do not chase it; you'll be lost if you do.

Instead, stay the course. Close your eyes, play with eyes open, be held accountable, play with others and share your experience.

Get qualified, experienced guidance to support you in going deeper and expanding. The state will take root as the Universe sees fit, and not before.

Until one has attained any degree of regular ability to keep present, living life in the now and developing a relationship with consciousness period it could even be seen as a distraction and more fodder for the ego.

Bear this in mind, I've seen so many more people learn about these things, memorize them, and tout them than those who actually attain embodiment of them. Don't be that unfortunate soul, Om-ie

The Physiology of an Awakened Human

This is a little really rudimentary Science behind what we are doing here - and maybe it has lit you up. This stuff totally lights me up!

GEEKY Yogic Science Freak here! I LOVE talking about this with people who are way smarter than I am so I can better articulate it to you. But I don't depend on what anyone says. I was having my own experience before I looked at some of the Science.

Scientific evidence is cool and fun in its affirmation - but I don't value it over what I am experiencing. I do value that which my own living conscious teacher directs me toward - as my own personal experience.

Science is about facts, numbers and the mind. It can inspire some folks to be open-minded enough to try something. Then I suggest letting your own experience be the thing that fuels you.

If you add meditation to your lifestyle *diet*, it will begin to produce the same standard results it does for everyone else, with some degrees of variation depending on the level of stress in your body, your life and in your own unique wiring.

Can you hang with me while I unpack some of this? This stuff juices me up!

Telomeres

Do you know what telomeres are?
They are a protective section of DNA at the end of certain chromosomes. Telomeres are responsible for maintaining integrity and stability of chromosomes.

The length of a telomere tells us how old the cell is and how much division it has left - in other words, telomeres are associated with aging. When a telomere shortens it is less protective of the cell.

Check this out. Current Science shows that consistent meditative practice lengthens telomeres, increasing longevity.
Amazing right?

Who knew that Meditation was the Fountain of Youth!

Telomeres also protect the cell from free-radical cells like cancer. Cells with short telomeres are more vulnerable than those with longer telomeres.

Neural Function

Do you know something about how the brain functions and creates neural connections, hardwiring, and how those things change?

There's a saying "neurons that fire together, wire together." These are pathways of communication in the brain. The energetic messages move through the neuron firing in a synapse.

When this is habituated over time, a fatty layer forms around the two neurons making an insulated hardwire.

It was once believed that hardwiring was what it was and we couldn't change it. We had the wrong map once again.

Meditation can change hardwiring.

Where once there was a neural pathway that led us into self-destructive tendency, we now choose peace. Where once there was a neural pathway that led us to anger quickly, we now find ourselves at peace. Where once we couldn't manage our checkbook, we now find we are intuitively able. Where once we saw praise as a threat, we now glow and receive it graciously.

The myelin sheaths around new habitual firing are filled with the baseline of gratitude, innocence, being totally in the flow and passionately alive, feeling absolute purpose, passion, peace, joy, love and grace.

Neurotransmitters + Protein Molecules

There are many different neurotransmitters. These are protein molecules which determine many things about our experience of life, our health, longevity, vitality, attention span and therefore our ability to be present.

In the typical waking state of consciousness there is an abundance of cortisol and adrenaline.

These molecules are not bad or harmful on their own. It is the abundance of them and the lower percentages of some of the other neurotransmitters that creates distress and disease, as well as the inability to be present.

When we meditate regularly and cultivate the ability to be present, these "stress" hormone protein molecules lessen in percentage and we see an increase in different neurotransmitters and neuropeptide molecules.

Serotonin, Melatonin, Endorphins like Dopamine and Oxytocin, GABA, DHEA (the longevity molecule), as well as growth hormone are all increased in regular meditators!

That may mean nothing to you right now, so let's look at what these do for us...

Neurochemicals

Serotonin - neurotransmitter regulating mood, sleep and digestion. This is the "happy" hormone I talk about often.
When we meditate the brain floods and bathes in Serotonin. We then have a much greater capacity to experience happiness for no reason at all.

Endorphins - in the Opioid neuropeptide family, buffering stress, providing soothing and pleasure, reducing pain.

Meditation increases endorphins reducing our pain and provides us with a natural chemical buffer between us and stress.

Oxytocin - neuropeptide promoting nurturing behaviors and bonding.

Meditation increases Oxytocin giving us the capacity to nurture, bond, love and receive more fully.

GABA - gamma aminobutyric acid, is a primary neurotransmitter responsible for inhibiting the receiving neuron.

A major lack of GABA is always found in those with chemical dependency. In one with low GABA you will see anxiety, nervousness, racing thoughts and sleeplessness.

In one hour of meditation GABA has been shown to increase by 27%

DHEA - known as the "longevity molecule" in our western world and is one of the most important hormones in the body.

In the general population, DHEA decreases year after year which produces aging. We see a dramatic increase of this molecule in yogis and meditators - literally reversing signs of age in the body.

Growth Hormone - produced during the Delta brain wave frequency - obtained in deep dreamless sleep and in meditation.

This positive impact on Growth Hormone gives meditation the title of "the fountain of youth".

Growth Hormone is made by the pituitary gland. Meditation has a positive, stimulating effect on this all-important gland in our brain positively influencing health on all levels.

There is more to this I won't get into here. Partly because I am a geek about this Science stuff, but not an expert.

Please go investigate for yourself if you desire to understand further.

The point is, meditation's effect on the body is incredibly positive, protective, and healing. That is something to celebrate and inspiration to get your eyes closed, right?

KeyPoints

★   No problem can be solved from the same level of consciousness that created it.

★   Evolution requires humans to enter into a new state of consciousness.

★   The state beyond waking, sleeping and dreaming is known by many names, we will call it the 4th. It is a state where we are both rested in the body but also alert in the mind.

★   This state can be accessed through many activities that we love - though not typically stabilized ever without a proper tool and experienced guidance to help one clearly re-establish life in the present moment.

★   Accessing and Stabilizing this 4th state changes the chemical soup in our body and rewires our brain so that we have a greater capacity to be and remain present, to be and remain happy and to be and remain as healthy as is possible for us.

★   It is possible for most anyone to access and stabilize this reality through the devoted, consistent use of meditation and consciousness exercises.

★ The world is shifting toward this new set-point for humans. The transition into this new world will be easier for individuals with these tools and stabilizing this state today.

Quest Goals

★ Close your eyes for one more time today than you have been and add an additional 3-10 minutes to your sessions.

★ Play with at least one of the consciousness exercises at least 3 times today. Pick your times. For example - at meal times, in the car, at a traffic light, on a bathroom break.

★ Consider the implications of developing higher states of consciousness in your own nervous system organically as you use these practices. What does this consideration do for you?

★ Consider what it would be like if 10% more people on the planet (or more) were consciousness developing higher states of consciousness. What would the potential implications be within homes, workplace, communities, countries, the human race?

The Awakened Human

We once thrived supernaturally exploring our miracle powers in the incredible reality of Vashti.
Vashti was a mildly temperate environment, rich with plants to eat and animals to befriend. There was peace. Beyond peace we knew ourselves to be expanding consciousness. We cared for the nervous system as a diving conduit for consciousness. We did not fear death. There was no concept of lack or control. There was perfect love and perfect trust. We lived in gratitude and harmony - vibrationally unable to ever drop beneath that frequency, only able to expand it beyond imaginings. We were in unified consciousness. We did not suffer nor struggle. We lived well.
A return to Vashti is predicted and imminent. The superhuman returns in this golden age of enlightenment.
We are being restored to the internal throne of the sovereign empress or emperor within. We telepathically, intuitively understand. We

embody spiritual evolution. We are living inside of a body with open meridian channels and chakras, a juicy pineal gland and attention fixed in the present moment.

We explore these super powers of the super human, in perfect balance, holiness and joy.

We usher in a world where having a psychic gift, the healer ability, the knowledge of plant medicines and of magic are commonplace.

A place where dancing to and making music, the practice and displays of the arts, the communion with and shared understanding of the cosmos and this amazing earth realm are all what is normalized.

Living in the now, today.
Vashti is restored on Earth.
We are leaving this legacy for generations to come.
Jai Ma

Fortification of Badassery

"It takes passion, and one-pointedness, and an absolute commitment to keep going until the job is done, until you have the actual living experience that there is no limitation or separation and that we are all One." -Maharishi Krishnananda Ishaya

As we progress we might like to know how to track our progress, how to continue to set ourselves up for success, how to go further and continue our growth of living life present.

What I Would Do

So what would I do having been someone who's gone before you?

★   I would find an excellent meditative tool to help me become clear about the present moment, to heal my nervous system and rewire my brain.

★   I would find a community of people who were endeavoring this awakening, stabilizing it, and excited to serve humanity in waking up to this reality.

★   I would find experienced, qualified guidance that resonated with me to help me to utilize those tools and guide me in my own growth.

★   Be teachable. I would ask for help. I would ask for reflection. I would use the tools every single day as often as possible, and I would ask for feedback about what I'm experiencing, what I think I'm supposed to be experiencing, what my doubts or what my fears are.

★   Be very innocent like a child, very honest like a child as I approached my teacher or my mentor about what is happening for me in my life. I would be vulnerable and try not to spiritualize it, not try to make it look pretty. I would be raw and authentic.

★ I would also make sure that those I joined forces with were reverent, experienced, and no - nonsense, but also people who have a lot of fun. I'd look for people living with passion, joy, love and authenticity.

★ I would do it right now and not wait another breath, another day. Because I know some of the implications of people staying in the drone states and I know the potential implications of people waking up, adding to that collective wakefulness of humanity - it's no small difference.

That's the level of Badassery that I'm talking about, people.

If you've gotten to this point in the book, well done. ***Congratulations! I think you're amazing and I'm so glad that you're here.***

If you have been doing the Quest Goals, following the suggestions, and doing your practices then kudos to you! You are in the top 1% at this time.

The magic starts to wear off for anyone though, my friends.

Finishing the book or doing what it takes to bolster yourself making this a lifelong journey of aliveness and presence, becomes less of a priority so quickly that you could easily fall out of the 1% at any time unless you protect your interests now. I have seen it with thousands of people.

Look around you. You know that it's true.

People start things all the time and they don't finish them. They don't see it through to the end, don't follow through on their dreams, their goals, their plans because it gets hard, doesn't it?

When it gets hard and we don't have a plan, we will abandon our endeavor. When we don't know what to do, don't have community, and don't have guidance, we give up, and we go back to the drone state - because it's what we do know how to do. It's familiar and it's comfortable. You've done it yourself as have I.

I'm going to tell you that it's OK to give up, to fall off this wagon for a moment or a day. But you don't have the luxury of staying there.

If you know in your heart that you were one of the people who's here to shift consciousness, you don't have that kind of luxury nor that kind of time.

You must begin to exercise this new muscle of consistency, of follow-through, because inertia and gravity are too great if you don't protect and prioritize this endeavor.

At least 1% of you will establish life in a higher state of consciousness and see this thing through until humanity itself fully wakes up.

Wherever you are on the spectrum of interest in this, you are welcome here. You will be able to help others no matter what level of interest you have. Your presence is important.

Practicing these techniques and sharing them with others is important. Developing a relationship with the present moment is important.

Your growing community and teaching others how to be playful with this experience is important. It doesn't matter whether you're just interested in developing a meditation practice or in becoming more present, or if you are wanting to teach these things to others, or if you want to fully awaken into full human consciousness and serve humanity in the awakening.

We are all in the same sandbox. We are all on the same adventure, and we are all adventurers here with necessary roles to play.

Thank you so much for your time and attention- your presence is precious and I am so grateful to have you engaging in our community and in these practices. You are helping to add to the collective vibe of awakening. The Angels are singing!

If you choose to continue from this moment forward, I admire your grit, your determination, your courage, your willingness and your sense of adventure. When you don't feel like it, you'll do it anyway for the good of humanity.

You recognize how you are the sovereign in your story - your own hero or heroine. You choose that level of responsibility for your consciousness and take a similar responsible stance for how your consciousness impacts humanity.

You're also understanding that while you are sovereign and responsible, you are never alone. We are in this thing together, in solidarity. The Angels and Ascended beings who went before us are right here too.

Heck - the whole Universe is listening and supporting this endeavor now. It has always been serving you to awaken.
It's designed to fail you when you make the wrong things a priority and it's designed to give you everything to support you in your role for the enlivening of consciousness.

As you proceed, if you do, you will come to feel and know this as your own experience. No need to believe me.

Mythic Badassery Moving Forward

Change- it's not some overwhelming thing you have to swallow. It's small steps, bite sized pieces - a practice of becoming, of trading one habit for another - that's all. And you do not have to do it alone.

Make YOUR real life a mythic adventure. Fall into fascination with it. There is no one else's life that should be more compelling to you.

Let this book and all that comes along with it inspire you into possibility, but especially into action. Live into a curious exploration as you employ the suggestions.

Create rituals for recognizing how amazing your life is. Choose to fall in love with the adventure you are on. Even if in making this choice, you aren't in love at first, you will find greater and greater magic, adventure and aliveness.

Practice living life from that loving, grateful, awe-filled vantage point. Practice celebrating your life. Notice and be innocent with the elements of your life and the people in your life. You can feel it as Epic. Riveting. Alive.

The fact that you are here suggests that you've been pulled forward by the part of you that KNOWS and longs for Passionate Aliveness.

You may have been too asleep, too inundated with all you do to keep yourself busy, too stubborn to notice that part of you beckoning you to return. It has always been here though.

Is applying what you learn here revealing even a wee smidge of passionate aliveness? Does your mythic adventure feel more badass?

Notice Your Up-Leveling

If you have done the work, implementing and meeting Quest Goals along the way, then you have faced modifications, faced ability checks, earned character victories, gained some proficiency and begun to up-level your range of possibility.

As you have practiced consistency - a crucial element in success on your Adventure, you've begun to finally really get somewhere with the meta, maha, keystone ability to be present.

How's that going for you? Do you see your growth? Can you see how the "hit points" of life and the moments of modification, reassessment, of coming back to the moment or to your practice have all been an integral, inextricable part of your Adventure?

Do you see how it's all developed character? Take a moment to really drink that in.

Failing forward, feel the fear and do it anyway. It's not failure - it's strengthening the muscle of consciousness. Don't waste a second judging any part of it.

You might like to know that you aren't qualified to judge it anyway. You aren't omniscient enough. Might just as well line up with the congruence of your true nature, follow the map, engage with the other Adventurers and keep going rather than waste a second on judging.

The Next Level Up

You are growing in your capacity to be and remain present. You will see this organically unfold, but you can also participate in the upleveling.

Word of caution - don't chase this down, people, or you will be immediately stuck.

You can not control it, but rather, be a willing conscious participant in it - awake enough to do what is suggested, to cultivate the right conditions for your upleveled badassery to emerge, as well as to be present enough to the fact that the upleveling is occurring.

Here is where reflection from others and gratitude are useful. By reflection, I mean the Universe reflecting to you how you are growing and changing.

You can also participate with this by writing a gratitude list each day or each week for how you see these quest goals and practices in this book are infiltrating the experience of life. Even if you see some things falling apart, you can be sure it is the element of Grace that comes to line life up for you to be awake more, stay awake longer, expand the capacity to enjoy life optimally, and to be of service in this world.

In order to level up, you have to be willing to continue doing what you've already been doing, reevaluate it, make tweaks and changes as needed, ask for help, ask for honest reflection, consider honestly what is working and what isn't working and what the solution might be to get you on track, keep you on track to deepen and expand the experience and to otherwise keep going.

Perspective

For me, I've needed to accept the fact that growth is not linear, that we don't just get from point A to point B to point C on to point Z in the way that we've often been taught. Point A to B to C can sometimes look very linear.

By the time we arrive at point D & E it can look like we're going backwards, like we've fallen off the wagon, like we've become distracted, like life is happening too much for us to stay on track.

In truth this is just a part of the process of life's unfolding and we can welcome it in like we welcome in the thoughts, the emotions, and any other diversion - as a part of our practice.

In order for me to remember that these diversions, these distractions, these seeming back steps are a natural part of the process of awakening, of life, of meditation, of consciousness, I have needed experienced guidance. I have needed peers who are walking the same path as I am. I have needed structure and support to turn to consistently.

I have needed to take myself out of my life, out of society, for long periods of time and short periods of time in order to gain the experience of meditation, of consciousness technique, of practicing staying present without the diversions and distractions of daily life.

I have required all of the above in order to establish an awesome, unwavering, flawless, doubtless foundation which has led me into deeper, richer, more expanded experiences of the present moment, of my true nature, of being awake sustainably.

That may not be your style of path. But taking yourself out of the regular routine of daily life occasionally to attend workshops, retreats and training that will assist you in going further, faster. The right guidance and support empowers you into doubtlessness and therefore clarity in choosing for being present. This makes you a more useful and effective human.

What I find is when a person does not have this kind of commitment and support, they ultimately wind up listening to the voice in their head, identifying it as their own spiritual guru in there. Once that happens, they compromise and inevitably choose to enter back into the path of the drone - as opposed to the awakened Jedi state.

Therefore, it seems like doing some kind of training and having some kind of support is essential for one to really be able to transcend the habits of the mind.

A Different Kind of Adventurer

It may be that all you're meant to do is read this book, practice a few of the exercises and get on with your life. That's great and absolutely of value in and of itself.

But for some of you, you know that you're here for *something more*. You really don't just want to establish a regular, consistent meditation practice and you don't just want to learn how to re-establish life in the present moment.

You want to see "how far the rabbit hole goes." You are hungry to tap into and unleash the spiritual potential within you. You can feel the reality of higher states of consciousness and what zesty aliveness, what elements of Badassery await you.

It's helpful to know that where once it seemed these experiences seemed only for the precious few - those who went to sit in caves on the mountain or in monasteries, that is not the case.

While it is commonly known that someone who is "enlightened" doesn't talk about it or feel the need to say so, my testimony and purpose for writing this book has been to inform you that it is time we all claim this possibility.

It is time we prioritize the journey into it. We can't afford to be coy. There is great upheaval in our world as this transition from unconsciousness to consciousness takes place.

It will feel less chaotic for you and you will make it less so for others if you align with this adventure. You have a destiny here. There are people waiting behind you for you to establish life lived in the present moment, in a higher state of consciousness, so that they then can too.

For you, my kindred spirit, you absolutely must enlist the support of community and guidance in addition to employing these tools. And you'll be the ones who will do it because that fire is obvious in you.

The time of the sage in the cave high in the Himalayan mountains is over. The time for Christ or Buddha consciousness to dawn within so many human hearts has been here for some time now.

It's your turn to come clear and embody this. You are meant to exercise the muscle of living into those states and stabilize them. It is time to be a true transmitter of passionate aliveness, inner freedom and grace. You are here to wake up and to help others remember that that's why they're here too.

I have become a living example of some degree of this, as have my peers, mentors and teachers. In fact there are many people on the planet now who are on this path, who are on this mission, who are living into these higher states of consciousness.

If that resonates for you, I urge you to find the things that you think might be in your way. Investigate those limitations and change your focus in life.

KeyPoints

★   What it takes to succeed is desire, a clear why, willingness to keep going, refinement of practice through guidance, playmates in this sandbox, courage, grit, determination, inspiration, renewed commitment, continual education.

★   You are the change you've been waiting for.

★   If you are resonating with and feeling passionate about waking up - consider taking next steps to support your practice (close and open eyes) and to what degree your heart is ready to take this right now. Be willing to be bold.

Quest Goals

★   Consider how to take your practice to the next level, both close eyes and open eyes. Make it measurable, schedule it, then do it.

★   Consider at least one area you continue to trip up in - whether it's something that happens with your eyes closed, in getting your eyes closed, or in not remembering to come present with eyes open. Write about why you think it is that you're having this difficulty.

★ Now that you've journaled about this area of difficulty, break it down into just a basic essence of that storyline.

For example if it's that you continue to feel too busy to sit down and close your eyes, the essence of that storyline is that you don't feel like you have permission to sit down and close your eyes.

Or maybe it's that you feel guilty coming present with eyes open doing the consciousness exercises while in conversation with people because you feel that you aren't being present with them by using the technique as opposed to not.

Your base issue here would be feeling like you don't have permission to be present in the middle of conversation.

★ Now that you've journaled and considered in a refined way what you're struggling with share this with the group. If you can't get down to your base issue, ask for support with that in the Facebook group so that a member of our team with experience and qualification can help guide you to both meet and overcome this challenge.

★ Journal about where you feel you're at on the spectrum of what your role is in this adventure.

For example you might know already that you want to be in the 1% and see humanity wake up to heaven on earth.

Or you might just be here to learn meditation and how to be present.

Wherever you're at on the spectrum, journal about your role and then let us know - shamelessly and proudly, what you've discovered. Everyone in every role is needed and welcomed here.

★ Have you ever felt you were here to do something special? Do you sense that now?

★ Where in your life do you not act like the sovereign hero in the adventure of your life?

Take Me All the Way Home

In the wake of all that seemed real,
I woke to find only One thing is.
I dance in and out of this clarity.
Let me come all the way Home.
Moments where I am asleep wandering,
Certain this illusion is real,
Let me come all the way Home
and remain here.
Let me be kind and compassionate knowing
Oneness with the parts of me that still sleep.
This wakefulness, I see, is not for me.
It seems to be for the rest of You, Lord, that
has not yet remembered.
Take me all the way Home.
As every part is restored.
Amen

Ultimate Purpose

"Let my idle chatter be the muttering of prayer, my every manual movement the execution of ritual gesture, my walking a ceremonial circumambulation, my eating and other acts the rite of sacrifice, my lying down prostration in worship, my every pleasure enjoyed in dedication of myself, let whatever activity is mine become form of worship of you." - Adi Shankaracharya

**"Seek ye first the Kingdom of Heaven, and all else shall be added unto you."
- Jesus the Christ**

Humanity is at a holy precipice. It is the 12th hour. People are waking up and joining in the manifestation and the recognition of heaven on earth.

Not in an airy fairy, exalted kind of way, but in a very embodied, alive, rich, exquisite, very human, very present, sort of way. A daring and crucial focus for you might be the good in mankind.

You could look at it as the holiness or the consciousness in humans. This kind of focus would include you speaking, thinking, and acting in alignment with these notions as truth.

It would be one where you see yourself as an agent for holiness and never leave the inner throne, the present moment, for anything.

It would be one where you have a stake in the ground for that kind of reality. It would be a bold life as compared to what most of us have lived inside of trying to be cool, to fit in, to survive - connecting with other humans in such shaky, flimsy, surfacey ways as suffering, stress, and compromise.

Instead of commiserating in bitching, gossiping, complaining and the like, we inspire one another to remain present and notice the magic and wonder, the glory of our existence. We empower one another. We are shameless and generous with our own presence.

This kind of life provides us with dignity and humility. We evolve into advanced beings transmitting the highest frequencies of love, pure consciousness and passionate aliveness.

No one is wasting energy drawing lines in the sand or trying to be understood. No one is fighting for or against anything. People are living fully so there is no time for that nonsense.

There is a prophecy which states that it is to come. I am here living inside of the magic of evolution into that, and it's all I see. I call it *heaven on earth* and more is revealed every day.

I recognize some of you who have been answering this call, and I stand with those who are clearly inside of it, welcoming you. Thank God you are finally here - and yet, we know it is right on time.
Do you feel that tingle?

The Initiation

Throughout history men and women have always had initiation portals. In all indigenous cultures in every area of the world, throughout all of time, there has been a way for men and women to ceremonially acknowledge rites of passage.

Specifically, when one aligns with one's spiritual purpose and destiny, when one is ready to accept responsibility for their own spiritual journey and be of service to something greater than themselves, a ceremony takes place.

In this ceremony, one is initiated, oftentimes taking a certain set of vows or taking on a certain set of boundaries, to assist one in living life purely aligned with a specific purpose and mission.

In this lifetime, I have been privileged to be formally initiated as a priestess and as a monk. I have also been blessed to walk the path of officiant and initiator.

Initiation ceremony is a beautiful, deeply stirring and ancient way to make a clear commitment to and send a clear message to the universe about your heart's desire, your life's mission, your spiritual intention.

There is an intensity, sacredness, a sense of aliveness. Initiation gives a sense of being supported by the unseen forces of the universe. It gives a sense of deeply, richly feeling in absolute communion with this *something more* that one is lining life up with.

Exercise

You will need a journal or notebook, something to write with, some quiet space and maybe a candle if you have one and can light it.

Begin by lighting your candle if you are using one. Consider this as turning on the energy of initiation.

Relax your body. Engage and empty into the present moment. Allow for the rise and fall of the breath coming and going, and anything else that is, to be exactly as it is.

Do this for several rounds of breath until you are feeling completely centered and relaxed.

Now let awareness be wide. Notice how held you are by gravity and all of the spaciousness surrounding you. Notice your own presence.

Open to the pulse of aliveness.
This may come as your own body pulse, the breath or a subtler pulse from the ethers. Consider this pulse a form of support from consciousness right now.

Open to the idea that sentinel-like beings of light, standing in observance of humanity - come closer, paying more attention here.

These beings exist in service to humanity's awakening, and they are ready and willing to assist you as you move forward with your commitments and with your practice. They are ready to help you hit the reset button and recommit to your path, to your journey into the present moment, and the journey into stabilization of higher states of consciousness. They are here to support you as you begin serving others.

Can you feel that? Does that feel alien for you, or does that feel completely resonant for you? Allow space for any discomfort. Rest more deeply. Be all here now.

Consider your personal commitment - to meditate and be present more regularly, to awaken higher states of consciousness, to serve others.

Write down the essence of your personal commitment to continue your practice of meditation, your practice of being present, and whatever else you are now called to share.

Make it specific and doable. Make it measurable and time bound. Make it applicable to the subject matter here.

Read it to yourself and tweak it if need be. When you are content that you've clarified a clear commitment, read it out loud to the unseen support surrounding you.

When you are complete, bow your head, hands in Anjali (prayer) mudra and be still, giving silent thanks.

Blow out your candle.

A Formal Vow Option

The following can be done alone or with a companion. This is for folks who feel very called to wake up and serve others in waking up.

This is a Buddhist vow known as the *Vow of the Bodhisattva*. There are many versions. This version is from the Upaya Zen Center and Jack Kornfield, a well-known Zen Buddhist teacher.

You should feel free to change the wording in a way that is meaningful for you. I suggest you include yourself in the "all" part of this vow.

Light a candle or sit in a beautiful natural scene.

Do a brief period of meditation and feel deeply into your own center. Have this or some version of these vows with you to read aloud.

The Vow:

Creations by Suffering Beings are numberless, I vow to free them all

Delusions are inexhaustible, I vow to transform them all

Reality is boundless, I vow to perceive it

The Awakened Way is unsurpassable, I vow to embody it

When you are complete pause to feel the essence of what you've just done.

Guided Vow Option

For your own guided initiation into being made useful to humanity's awakening, visit the website rodasicampbell.com and under ReSources choose the post called *The Initiation.*

Once you've given yourself this gift, take a few moments to write what your experience was - whatever is true for you is welcome.

I want you to write about it, and then if you feel so inclined, share with us in the **Rock Your Mind Global** Facebook group.

Lastly I want to invite you to imagine what it would be like to have a real live initiation ceremony lining up with such a thing in this lifetime.

It's a very real probability if you stick around that you could have such an experience of committing yourself to the path of presence, to the path of remaining in the zest of this adventure, into Badassery, into higher states of consciousness, and in service to others.

If that would be of interest to you, I would encourage you to examine our retreats or training program offerings. They will vary from time to time. Find out what's happening real time for you.

Another option is to connect with us and co-create an experience together should you feel your heart being pulled forward by that idea.

The *Rock Your Mind* mission is to empower individuals to cultivate, fortify and celebrate a state of Badassery. It's about guiding, encouraging, training and otherwise serving individuals who wish to grow and seek a community to play alongside of.
We are here to serve those who are awakening to their own mythic adventure, their own responsibility within that adventure, and their own heart's desire to assist others in turn to awaken.

That will look different for each individual. We need conscious parents, conscious firefighters, conscious doctors, conscious lawyers, conscious teachers, conscious surfers, conscious builders, conscious you name it.

You can be a part of this by reading this book or you can take it way beyond as far out as you can go. It's all welcome.

Holy Adventure

A sense of direction in life is not a plan nor a "my desires" list. Instead, it's the Holy Adventure and it is out of your control and so exciting!

The BEST ever guide is taking you here and there, bringing you this person and that experience, all for you to be awake, to praise, be grateful for, marvel at, expand because of, love and serve. It all comes. All comes to you. This is the truth.

And Purpose? You have always known what your highest, ultimate purpose is.

Don't make that complex.
Don't let ego manage it.

Your ultimate purpose is to rest in inner silence and watch as you passionately and unwaveringly begin to live life from there.

Whatever your unique dharma is will be obvious and come to you. You don't have to go looking for it. Cultivate the willingness to allow, to surrender when you are not allowing, and the habit of humbly asking for help when you can not do that.

Be present enough to see subtle and not-so subtle promptings from Shakti Flow. The promptings are always here. You've developed a strong muscle of ignoring it because someone you loved or liked a lot teased you about your unique special sweetness and it hurt - so you grew to protect it, deny it, and so, too forgot.

Be committed, gentle, and determined to allow yourself to be freed. The mind has stopped you from noticing your own eternal nature. Your addiction to the mind has stopped you from allowing passionate aliveness, badassery to emerge. Your relationship to the mind is changing now. That is something to celebrate!

Now Thriving

Thriving, not surviving, is your destiny and purpose. I don't know about your financial situation. I don't know about your body or health situation.

But I do know that if you practiced being present and giving your life to that more of the time than you have been, you will experience a state of thriving internally that you've never experienced before and maybe didn't even dream was possible.

Your desire for this experience is everything. Followed by your devotion to practice. Without those two things this isn't going to work. Keep in mind that this adventure doesn't end until you die and therefore the practice, the engagement, all of the support, all of the service doesn't stop until you die either.

This is a non-linear journey into stabilizing life lived in the present moment and into a life filled with unconditional love, passionate aliveness, and causeless bliss.

This is my experience. You aren't going to know what to expect next. That used to freak me out. It is pretty awesome now.

Final Sentiments

What I would do next is to keep going. I would keep going with practice. I would keep going with communication. I would keep going with support. I would keep going with growing and learning. I would keep going with vulnerability and innocence and authenticity.

If your personal commitment is not up yet and you finished the book, way to go and keep going!

If you've passed your mark but have completed the book, awesome, well done, way to go.

If you've read the book and not completed all of the Quest Goals, go back through and complete them.
If you've completed any of the Quest Goals, well done, you rock. Now go back and do the rest of them.

If you've read the book and done some of the Quest Goals but you haven't been engaged in our Facebook community, please give us the pleasure of getting to know you, of supporting you and of being inspired by you.

If you've not yet gone to the website and used any of the resources or participated in any of the classes inside of the Facebook page - please do yourself a favor and get the most out of what this book stands for, has to offer and beyond.

I look forward to getting to know you and growing with you and serving you and your own expansion and stabilization.

Bless you on your journey into meditation, into the present moment, and into seeing the way that you have stood between you and everything you've been looking for by being so conscious of your relationship to your mind, your emotions and circumstances.

Bless you as you recognize your own divinity, the ease of the present moment, the many blessings of this path and the way it bleeds out into every area of life and everyone you know and love and meet.

Bonus: A way to serve and spread good vibes...

"The best way to find yourself is to lose yourself in the service of others." - Mahatma Gandhi

First of all Om-ie, your practicing meditation and being present is a service to humanity - starting with your own mind/body, those around you and your community.

You are adding to the awakened rather than the drone part of consciousness. This is no small thing. Please remember this.

If you feel called to do something in a practical way to serve, here are some suggestions to help me share the LOVE.

- Give this book an honest positive review on Amazon or anywhere.
- Share a testimonial with me at the **Rock Your Mind Global** Facebook Group or email me from my website.
- Help me to fill our Facebook lives, blog, vlog and courses with relevant and useful material stemming from your own personal questions, challenges, and ahas! Ask away!
- Share your experience with this material with those you love and know in whatever way you are called to serve others in getting resourced.

Okay, Kindred Spirit

We are coming to the end of this particular book, but it's just the beginning of some really spectacular possibilities, and I've been so honored to get to serve you and thrive in consciousness with you here.

Jai Ma + Rock on and keep in touch, People!

KeyPoints

★   Your Ultimate purpose is to be present to Life. This is the Ultimate Gift and Service as well.

★   To be present to Life you have to commit to your practices. Commit to living your Holy Adventure.

★   Initiation is a personal way to formalize your commitment.

★   As you stabilize the experience of life lived in the present moment you make it easier for others to do so.

Quest Goals

★ Go get your eyes closed - amp it up a notch if you can.

★ Play with eyes open. Practice coming present whenever you think of it. Use the exercises in this book to help you with that.

★ Do the Initiation exercise in this chapter. Share about it.

★ Journal on: How can I keep going? How will I prioritize and schedule my continued growth and stabilization in this endeavor?

★ Keep Going and Spread the Love.

Epilogue: Channeling the Ascended Master - Sadashiva

We've been watching and holding the possibility of awakening for humanity always. With every cycle of creation there is a dawning and an ignorance that has repeated itself - or seemingly so.

That story - that appearance, is an illusion. There is only wakefulness.

That is what any soul comes into human form to discover. It is so attractive, so captivating, however, that many and most never even begin to seek it. Even fewer discover it and give everything to that.

These tides now shift, as we have held steadily this possibility and inevitability, for this appointed moment in humanity.

You, your soul imprint - is indeed one that has been journeying lifetime after lifetime attempting to awaken. Some of you have achieved it, now returning to set all free.

But the belief in awakening, too must be surrendered and dissolved in the fires of pure awareness. In you this must happen so that the rest of humanity may follow suit.

This sounds paradoxical, we know. But from the perspective of a free being, it is not.

You must choose the path of conscious awakening even to be able to surrender it. The same with everything else to be truly transcended. And so, you are to awaken - soon.

The scales of conscious awakening are tipping for all. You must re-cognize that you are not separate and this has nothing to do with you personally.

If you choose to remain mostly asleep, another nervous system will play the role. It is time now.

Never forget that the destiny of this lineage in some part, hinges on your interaction, engagement, service and most of all - your own surrender of self. Things can not work any other way.

Yet, others can't continue their own full awakening without yours, others who have yet to really understand what that means won't come to the realization unless you do.

Now make a clear choice and keep going. Surrender fully and keep going.

Meditation leads to being present to life; it leads to states of higher consciousness. If higher states of consciousness are possible and accessible - why would one not move toward cultivating, exploring and stabilizing that?

The purpose of cultivating higher states of consciousness is not for selfish means of more egoic delusion. It is solely for the purpose of serving others to discover the same - so that all humans may be awake and evolving more quickly and stably beyond the modern chaotic human existence.

There may be a secondary reason - and that is pleasure. Not the sort that one might think. It is not the pleasure of the individual self - although it may be experienced that way in earlier stages of consciousness. It is for the celebration and enlivenment of God's praise of God's creation. It is pleasurable to God, to the Universe, that humans awaken.

The majesty of this magical world is waiting to be revealed and enlivened with your attention. Humans waking up out of the state of striving, struggling, efforting, posing, trying and surviving - into a state of grace and bliss is what the Universe wants.

If one is meditating for any other reason, that is fine, but you need to know that the entire Cosmos is wanting to wrap you in your destined shroud of it's Love - for you to recognize that it already has done so. It is waiting for you to settle into your destiny and stay still therein.

Some of you won't be ready to align with this notion or vibration just yet, and that is to be expected. You can still gain immense benefit improving your individual sense of life by applying the practices and principles herein.

But some of you are ready and have been giving a lot of your energy already to awaken. For you, it is time to let go of all you think you know.

You can not take any of that with you where we are headed. Through the eye of the needle nothing but your awareness will fit through - and your pure authentic essence is only capable of passing through. No concept will fit.

Put down the spiritual robes and masks you don. Allow for things to be even more simple and alive. The state of "I know" does not fit through that eye of the needle.

Only awe, innocence, curiosity, willingness - only your burning desire can usher you through. This burning desire is not even "yours" - it is the Holy Spirit.

You are being prompted by your true self to return to your true home. This should be a relief. To your ego, when it is time to notice where you are afraid to let go, you will need to remember this. You will need to ask for help. You will need to return to open-mindedness, even if it angers you. Even if you are terrified.

It is in those fires that you'll be restored, invariably and eventually returned to the kingdom of heaven, here and now, in this human form, upon this earth, awake, and transmitting god-consciousness.

How one practices the path of consciousness - whatever tools one uses to train the mind - to take awareness and senses within, is important. You must be sure you have experience, qualified, time-tested practices and guidance. You can not get there by yourself.

We see so many who are caught in the path of exalted spiritual illusion and in the path of fixing, healing and dabbling in magic in every part of this mind-created universe. These folks go on for decades and more often entire lifetimes never transcending and never actually stabilizing the state of unified consciousness.

The tools you choose should be time-tested and show a track-record for this outcome.

Tools that keep you planning and visualizing a better life for the separate you and to enhance the mind-created level of reality, are completely insufficient for this end. They are completely adequate and effective for other things - but not for the path of stabilizing unified conscious awakening.

Humanity has finally come to the precipice and this is the time foretold. It is the heated up point and the 12th hour.
We are excited for you.

If you are enmeshed in effort and struggle and suffering and feeling like you are getting somewhere and then not and the ups and downs of the waking state of consciousness, then you are in a mind-created hell.

But if you are experiencing any degree of that and you are here, then never fear!

Stick around and employ what is offered here - drink deeply and keep observing what happens as you give this all you've got - you will begin to transcend that state quickly.
The world needs this from you.

Ascendant Master Sadashiva

Acknowledgements

To you, I do give thanks...
Maharishi Krishnanada Ishaya - without your guidance I'd still be wandering aimlessly in my head. Thank you for holding me in perfection as I dissolve in Divine Presence. Words can not express my gratitude and respect for you and your commitment to Consciousness.

To my teacher's teacher, Sadashiva - you who have guided me beyond the veil in the exploration of the Art of Ascension.

To my goddess girls, Lauren + Elora - your beautiful powerful souls grace me immeasurably. May you come to embody the essence of the Teaching of the One more fully than I ever do in this lifetime or beyond.

To Jackie, Sharon, Robin, Kathryn + Daniele.

To Satta, Narain, Manyu, Jaya and all Ishayas of the Bright Path.

To the BIG Ishayas beyond basic human perception, always holding the outcome of full human consciousness and LOVE.

To my family and friends who have supported this writing journey - my Angel Christopher, my Mother Dale Jean, Cori + Jesse Smoker, Jabo + the Bihlman Tribe, my sober family, the *Rock Your Mind* Love Tribe, my Priestess Soul Sisters and all students, family and friends who have continued to believe in me and show up for this work.

To Dharani Perdue + Jacki Erickson for your editing work, resources, advice and support + Robin Stremlow for the marketing magic.

Thank you for the love and guidance from the other side: Marianne + Leonard, Grandma Clara + Grandpa John and Grandma Jean + Grandpa Everett.

Deep Bow to all of my Germanic, Norse,
Indigineous Odawa North American and
other Ancient Ancestors.

About the Author

Rodasi Campbell is an International Speaker,
Channel, Coach + Author based out of
Traverse City, MI. She is an initiated monk,
and priestess, a sober woman and a mom.

Rodasi has presented in front of thousands of
folks in 6 different countries, trained business
teams & non-profit organizations, led
numerous apprenticeships and training
programs and has been a guest teacher and
co-facilitator at dozens of retreats.

Follow Along:
rodasicampbell.com
Rodasi Campbell Meditation (FB biz page)
Rock Your Mind Global (FB group)
Rodasi Campbell on Patreon + YouTube

Made in the USA
Middletown, DE
15 March 2021

35006901R00190